E-Training and Development

Colin Barrow

T0341418

- Learn about the global benefits of e-training and development, how to extend the knowledge 'shelf life' of your company, and how to reduce barriers to entry of high-quality training materials for all organizations

- Covers realistic e-training and development for all sizes of company that delivers a profitable payback

- Case studies of success stories from IBM, Scottish Power, Yamatake Building Systems and Cisco Systems

- Includes key concepts and thinkers, a glossary of terms, a comprehensive resources guide, and a section of FAQs, as well as a 10-step program to making e-training and development work

TRAINING & DEVELOPMENT

11.03

≫EXPRESS EXEC.COM≪
essential management thinking at your fingertips

First Published 2003 by
Capstone Publishing Limited (a Wiley company)
8 Newtec Place
Magdalen Road
Oxford OX4 1RE
United Kingdom
http://www.capstoneideas.com

CIP catalogue records for this book are available from the British Library and the US Library of Congress

ISBN 1-84112-444-3

Printed and bound in Great Britain by CPI Antony Rowe, Eastbourne

Wiley also publishes its books in a variety of electronic formats. Some content that appears in print may not be available in electronic books.

Websites often change their contents and addresses; details of sites listed in this book were accurate at the time of writing, but may change.

Substantial discounts on bulk quantities of Capstone Books are available to corporations, professional associations and other organizations. For details telephone Capstone Publishing on (+44-1865-798623), fax (+44-1865-240941) or email (info@wiley-capstone.co.uk).

Contents

Introduction to ExpressExec

ExpressExec is a completely up-to-date resource of current business practice, accessible in a number of ways – anytime, anyplace, anywhere. ExpressExec combines best practice cases, key ideas, action points, glossaries, further reading, and resources.

Each module contains 10 individual titles that cover all the key aspects of global business practice. Written by leading experts in their field, the knowledge imparted provides executives with the tools and skills to increase their personal and business effectiveness, benefiting both employee and employer.

ExpressExec is available in a number of formats:

- » **Print** – 120 titles available through retailers or printed on demand using any combination of the 1200 chapters available.
- » **E-Books** – e-books can be individually downloaded from ExpressExec.com or online retailers onto PCs, handheld computers, and e-readers.
- » **Online** – http://www.expressexec.wiley.com/ provides fully searchable access to the complete ExpressExec resource via the Internet – a cost-effective online tool to increase business expertise across a whole organization.

» **ExpressExec Performance Support Solution (EEPSS)** - a software solution that integrates ExpressExec content with interactive
tools to provide organizations with a complete internal management
development solution.
» **ExpressExec Rights and Syndication** - ExpressExec content can
be licensed for translation or display within intranets or on Internet
sites.

To find out more visit www.ExpressExec.com or contact elound@wiley-
capstone.co.uk.

Introduction to E-Training and Development

» Why training and development matters.
» Why e-training and development matters even more.
» How the knowledge "shelf life" is declining rapidly.
» How globalization and technology are changing the way everyone works and consumes.
» Leveling the training and development playing field for small businesses, the lifeblood of growing economies.

Since Hertzberg's seminal work[1] on motivation, it has been common knowledge that the opportunity for advancement is one of the primary motivators of people in organizations. The link between personal, corporate, and national advancement and training and development is also easily demonstrated.

Higher education, for example, which can be seen as the pinnacle of the training process, is closely correlated with economic development – enrolment ratios in higher education average 51% in the high income OECD countries, compared with 21% in middle-income countries and 6% in low-income countries.[2]

Business recognizes the importance of training and development by spending over $60bn a year on it,[3] and there is evidence that expenditure pays off. According to a study conducted by the American Society for Training and Development,[4] when a sample of publicly-traded companies was split according to expenditure on training per employee, the companies with the higher expenditure had higher average net sales per employee and higher average annualized gross profit per employee than the companies with lower training expenditure.

But the key finding in this study from an e-training and development perspective was not so much to do with the payback from investing in training and development as with the revelation that the top performing companies trained 84% of their own workforce, whilst the rest averaged just 35%. Even for the organization enlightened by self-interest, the benefits accruing from training can be hard to harvest. Several major and relatively new problems face any training organization.

» Understanding that in the US the average duration of employment in one organization has shrunk from 25 years in 1950 to less than five years today, means that organizations face a formidable problem in delivering quality learning at a low enough cost to ensure a profitable payback.
» People need new knowledge at an ever-increasing rate. The stock of human knowledge doubles every five years and if current trends continue it is expected to double every 73 days.[5] This in turn means that training and development programs and their material content have an ever-diminishing shelf life, hence a potentially higher unit cost.

» Work and consumption was once a local experience. People lived near their workplace and consumed what was produced in the area. Since the Industrial Revolution, that has changed and with the advent of IT and the Internet, the pace of change has turned the world into a "global village." The first stage of this globalization was about driving costs down by moving production to low-cost areas of the world. The latest stage is about quality of service and adding value to goods and services in order to gain more competitive advantage. Calling an airline reservation service or a computer help-line may be routed to Ireland, Canada, or India, dependent only on the time of day in the caller's country of origin. The service standard is expected, and required, to be the same and the knowledge skills of these "global" workers has to be identical.

» Small companies are being created at a faster rate than at any period in recent history. These companies, unlike earlier generations of small businesses who confined their activities to their immediate locality, have to compete on a world stage. Such companies need access to high-quality training and development materials if they are to have any serious chance of surviving and prospering. There is certainly well-documented and longstanding evidence that the ones who do access training resources do gain these benefits.[6]

E-training and development enables organizations of any size and in any part of the world to enjoy the benefits of a skilled and well-trained workforce. The medium lends itself to allowing training material to be developed quickly, disseminated widely, and for costs to be spread over a larger base of users than with more conventional forms of training, such as those delivered in classrooms by a "warm" instructor.

In recent years, more and more companies have started incorporating e-learning – study and training mediated by IT – into their staff training programs. Over the last few years, for instance, IBM introduced e-learning on a widespread basis in its executive management and new-technologies training programs. By converting some 30% of its total menu of training courses to the e-learning system, the company has been able to train e-commerce technicians around the world in an impressively short time, and its total training costs are claimed to have fallen by $125mn over the year.

Using e-training and development systems, large companies have successfully extended the shelf life of their knowledge[7] and small companies have overcome barriers that would otherwise have impeded their entry into new markets.[8]

NOTES

1 Herzberg, F. (1968) "One More Time – How do You Motivate Employees?" *Harvard Business Review*, Jan – Feb, pp. 109–120.
2 Kuni, A. (2000) "Higher Education Through the Internet – Expectations, Reality, and Challenges." *Development and Co-operation*, no. 2, March, pp. 23–25.
3 Industry Report (1999), *Training Magazine*, October, pp.46–48.
4 American Society for Training & Development (ASTD) (1998), *The State of the Industry Report*.
5 DTI (2001), *The Future of Corporate Learning*, Department of Trade and Industry Report, London, p. 6.
6 Hills, G.E. & Narayana, C.L. (1989) *Profile Characteristics, Success Factors and Marketing in Highly Successful Firms – Frontiers of Entrepreneurship Research* (eds Brockhouse, R.H., Sr, Churchill, N.C., Katz, J.A., Kirchhoff, B.A., Vesper, K.H., & Wetzel, W.E.M, Jr) Babson College, Wellesley, Massachusetts.
7 Meinster, J.C. (1998) "Extending the Short Shelf Life of Knowledge." *T+D Magazine*, vol. **52**, no. 6, pp. 12–14.
8 Ivis, M. (2000) *Analysis of Barriers Impeding E-Business Adoption Among Canadian SMEs*. Canadian E-Business Opportunities Roundtable E-Business Acceleration Team, SME Adoption Initiative.

What is Meant by E-Training and Development?

» Defining training and development.
» Is learning different from training and development?
» Defining the "e".
» Should it really be "I" for Internet or "W" for Web-based training?
» Who drives e-training and development?

"Training," according to Martyn Sloman, author of *The E-Learning Revolution*, "is the process of acquiring the knowledge and skills related to work requirements using formal structured or guided means, but excluding general supervision, job specific innovations, and learning by experience." Whilst it's easy to agree with the first part of his definition, the thrust of the latter part is more obscure. Sloman's definition goes on to say, "training lies within the domain of the organization: it's an intervention designed to produce behaviours from individuals that have positive organizational results." He then defines learning as "the physical and mental process involved in changing one's normal behavior patterns and habits." "Learning," he claims, is distinct from training as it "lies within the domain of the individual."

The purpose of this definition seems to be to attempt to create a new subject area, substituting the word "learning" for "training." In a sense it is possible to suggest that training is merely the way in which instruction is conveyed; it supports learning, which is our internal way of processing information into knowledge. But in practice this is nothing more than semantics. People learn in many different ways, but those ways involve the use of some medium – be it a book, case study, simulation, exercise, lecture, video, or lecture – all of which are acknowledged as part of the trainer's armory.

Companies want their staff to become more proficient. They want their sales people to learn new skills, their technicians to assimilate information on new products and processes, and may even want some of their telesales support staff to become proficient in new languages. But the staff themselves may be equally keen for their employer to provide the opportunity to acquire new knowledge and may on occasions take the initiative themselves in finding ways to acquire such knowledge.

The real division is not between training and knowledge, or even between an individual's personal aspiration and an organization's needs. Rather, it lies between the immediate operational requirements of helping people to perform their current tasks in much the same ways – which can be described as training – and development, which is focused on personal and organizational growth relating to the knowledge, skills, and aptitude people need to do their next job, usually with greater responsibilities and rewards, or a different form of their current job.

Much of the literature, most of the products and services, and almost all of the supply chain in the sector uses the term "e-learning" to be synonymous with "e-training and development," as will the rest of this book.

WHAT ABOUT THE "e"?

Probably the most confusing aspect of this subject is exactly what the "e" stands for in "e-training and development." The easy answer is that it is all about "electronic."

Once technology is brought to bear, it becomes an "e-process." Elliot Masie[1], founder of the MASIE Center (see Chapter 9), an authoritative US think-tank in this field, has offered these alternatives:

» **"e" is for "experience"** – the business drivers for e-learning are about changing the character or experience of learning in the organization. A learner in an e-learning offering would have the options of time-shifting, place-shifting, granularization, simulation, and community support, to mention but a few. These are not necessarily all electronic, but go to the heart of evolving and increasing the experience level.
» **"e" is for "extended"** – with e-learning an organization should be able to offer an extension of learning options, moving from an event perspective to an ongoing process. The footprint of the e-learning experience would be larger in terms of time and would linger with the learners throughout their work life.
» **"e" is for "expanded"** – the opportunity to expand training offerings beyond the limitations of the classroom is incredibly exciting. Can we offer learning to all employees globally? Can we offer access to an unlimited number of topics? Can we not be constrained by our training budget when it comes to meeting an employee request for knowledge?

DOES THE INTERNET RULE?

"The Internet has begun to radically change the teaching of adults in the US who want to improve their skills or further their general education"

> *Garry S. Becker, 1992 Nobel Laureate and the man who is attributed with first using the term "human capital."*[2]

The Internet is a relatively new phenomenon and as yet has contributed little directly to the profit of shareholders in its sector. However, being unprofitable does not mean it is without influence. John Chambers, the chairman of Cisco Systems (see the case study in Chapter 7), is on record as telling the *New York Times* columnist, Thomas Friedman, "The next big killer application for the Internet is going to be education. Education over the Internet is going to be so big it is going to make e-mail usage look like a rounding error in terms of the Internet capacity it will consume."

There is no doubt that Web-based training, as training delivered over the Internet is commonly called, is a powerful factor as a delivery mechanism in e-training and development programs. It allows many of the values – such as low cost, wide reach, 24/7 availability, and interactivity – that we commonly associate as benefits of the e-process to be brought to bear on training and development.[3] But important as it is, the Internet is only part of the picture. Alistair Fraser[4] of Penn State University summed up the process of simply moving established classroom training onto the Internet with little thought as to how it should be adapted to suit the new medium, as "shovelware." That is perhaps a suitable dampener to the views of Cisco's chairman given above.

Other common elements of the e-training and development mix include: computer-based training (CBT); computer-based learning (CBL); computer-based instruction (CBI); computer-based education (CBE); Web-based training (WBT); Internet-based training (IBT); and Intranet-based training (also IBT) – all fairly self-explanatory terms. Less easily understood are terms such as "browser-based training," used to describe courseware that requires a Web-browser to access it, but which could be running from the Internet, a DVD, or a CD-ROM.

In fact, some training programs will pull content from a Website, a DVD, and a CD-ROM. These courses are sometimes called hybrids, or hybrid-DVD-CD-ROMs.

Distance learning, or distance education, also has many of the characteristics of e-learning, but is most often used to describe instructor-led Web-based education. To complicate matters further, some theorists divide e-learning into three distinct branches: computer-aided instruction (CAI); computer-managed instruction (CMI); and computer-supported learning resources (CSLR).

Less common terms used in the field include:

» **online training** – an all-encompassing term that refers to any training done with a computer over a network, including a company's intranet or local area network and the Internet;

» **net-based training** – same as online training;

» **desktop training** – any training delivered by computer at one's desk;

» **desktop videoconferencing** – a real-time conference using live pictures between two or more people on a network who communicate via computer;

» **interactive training** – an umbrella term that includes both computer-based and multimedia training;

» **computer-assisted instruction** – a term used more commonly in education for any instruction where a computer is used as a learning tool;

» **self-paced training** – training which is taken at a time and a pace determined by the user; often used for text or audio/video self-study courses, the term is now used by some organizations to include computer-based, Web-based, and multimedia training;

» **multimedia training** – an older, but still widely used, term that describes a type of computer-based training that uses two or more media, including text, graphics, animation, audio (sound/music), and video.

A SIMPLE DEFINITION

E-training and development can best be defined as using some form of technology to deliver training and other educational materials.

Along with a dozen related buzzwords, some of which have been described above, it is simply the latest, in-fashion, all-embracing phrase for training delivered by a number of means. In the past, these have included the use of mainframe computers, floppy disks, multimedia CD-ROMs, and more recently DVDs, and interactive videodisks. Currently, Web technology (both Internet and intranet delivery) has become the preferred delivery option, but already a new sub-branch, "m-learning," is creeping onto the scene – which involves training delivered on PDAs such as Handspring and Palm Pilot and *via* wireless devices such as mobile phones.

WHO DRIVES E-TRAINING AND DEVELOPMENT?

This is perhaps a more important question than "what is e-training and development?" All training and development should be rooted in the strategic purpose of the organization and be derived from a training and development needs analysis. The starting point is to look at the skills, knowledge, and attitudes that are needed for a person to do their job now and in the future, and at the needs of the organization for different skills, knowledge, and attitudes that may be needed in the future. The organization then needs to find a balance between training and developing people currently in the organization and simply adding those requirements to the profile of new recruits.

What has been happening in both the supply and demand side of e-training and development, particularly with regard to Web-based provision, is that the initiative has rested with the IT sections of the organization and with their counterparts in supply organizations. The result has been very little profit for either party. Where the subject is seen as part of the HR function, and not as a stand-alone, catch-all "wonder" as the Internet was during the dot.com boom, it will thrive. Elsewhere, it is proving a disappointing and distracting sideshow.

NOTES

1 Masie, E. "An E-Learning Journey" in Rosenberg, M.J. (2001) *The E-Learning Revolution*. McGraw-Hill, pp. 35–38.
2 *Business Week*, December 17, (1999), p. 40.

3 Closs, R.C., Humphries, R., & Ruttenbur, B.W. (2000) *E-Learning and Knowledge Technology – Technology and the Internet Are Changing The Way We Learn*. Sun Trust Equitable Securities.

4 Fraser, A. (1999) Opinions and Arts Section, *Chronicle of Higher Education*, vol. **48**, August, p. B8.

The Evolution of E-Training and Development

» E-training and development – revolution or evolution?
» The knowledge explosion.
» The global supply chain.
» The stages of evolution.
» Profitability – the acid test.

Today, described as the time of the IT revolution, the only industry that exists without benefit of IT is the training/education industry. In the last 100 years, every industry has significantly altered its corporate structure through cost reduction, efficiency, or large-scale expansion in order to preserve its very existence. In the retail industry, small retailers in towns have given way to large-scale stores such as Wal-Mart; small-town hamburger joints have been transformed into McDonalds outlets; and small clothing stores have been replaced by The GAP. However, throughout those last 100 years, nothing has changed in the training/education industry. It will be that very industry which will be the next to undergo change, as predicted by Kevin Oakes, president and CEO of Click2Learn.

The e-training and development industry has moved forward quickly since Oakes made this statement two years ago. Sales of IT training/education services worldwide were estimated at $21bn during 2000 and are forecast to be about $34bn by 2004. In the Asia-Pacific region, the estimate for the year 2000 is $1.9bn, and for 2004 $3bn.[1] (See Fig. 3.1.)

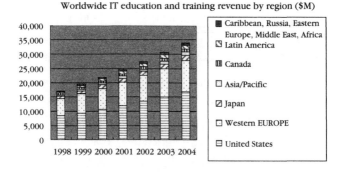

Fig. 3.1 Worldwide IT education and training revenue.

This forecast may not become a reality. The ASTD report for 2002[2] suggests that the high-water mark for the market may have been in 1997–8, with growth at best slowing down, but more likely leveling off. This same report, based on a survey of nearly 400 mostly American companies, confirmed that e-training and development was about 8% of total corporate expenditure on training, down from 9.1% in 1997. Declining enrollments were a result of negative experiences had with e-learning.

THE KNOWLEDGE EXPLOSION

For most of history, physical work has been the mainstay of economic life. The revolutionary turning points that have transformed the way people work include the following.

» Johann Gutenberg's invention of the printing press for movable type in 1435, which replaced centuries of handwritten paper-based communications, a method that restricted the flow of knowledge to a small, select group of people in any society.
» The agricultural revolution of the eighteenth century and the industrial revolution of the nineteenth century, which can be seen as the start of the need for knowledge-workers. Increasingly, workers left the land to work in factories with equipment and machinery that needed to be operated and maintained. These new jobs needed specialist skills rather than merely physical prowess. Workers had to have their skills updated to stay in work and the flood of immigrants had to be trained in the rudiments of the new jobs.
» The management revolution of the early to middle twentieth century changed the nature of work yet again. The year 1920 has been pinpointed as the point when the human resource function was born[3] and with it the advent of the formation of personnel departments whose purpose was "to get good employees and keep them."[4]
» The computer era which emerged during the 1950s fundamentally altered work patterns and brought with it the widespread requirement for a knowledgeable work force. The raw data in the US Census for the period 1900–1980[5] tells the full story. During that period, the percentage of farm-workers fell from 37.5% in 1900 to 2.8% in 1980. Those involved in manual and service work remained static at around 45%, but "white-collar" workers grew from 17.6% to 52.8% in less than a century. So knowledge-workers were born and with them came the urgent requirement for ways to disseminate existing knowledge efficiently and new knowledge quickly.

Organizations are dealing with a revolutionary need for knowledge by creating "knowledge repositories."[6] These are a combination of database and Web technologies which store and disseminate "knowledge objects," self-contained, reusable pieces of content that satisfy a specific performance-based learning object. This "internal" knowledge dissemination is possibly the most valuable aspect of the e-learning industry.

The thirst for better ways to disseminate knowledge is being spurred on by the following two major factors.

» The pace of business has increased dramatically and continues to accelerate. This makes it difficult to keep employees up to speed with new products and processes.
» The sheer amount of knowledge is growing and the "work-to-learn ratio" is being altered radically. The amount of time available is not growing, so either people have to work less and learn more or work even longer hours, and there is some evidence that this is happening. Or efficiencies have to be achieved in work or learning, or preferably both. The reward for more efficient knowledge dissemination is that the working day does not have to get longer.

THE GLOBAL SUPPLY CHAIN

Up until the mid-1950s, the world could be seen as one in which exporters and importers operated in a fairly traditional pattern. Cocoa, tea, rubber, and so forth were available in some parts of the world, whilst banking services, vehicles, and manufacturing equipment were available elsewhere. Countries erected trade barriers and tariffs to protect their own trade areas and relationships. With the General Agreement on Tariffs and Trade of 1947 (the GATT Treaty), governments and business turned their minds as to how to remain competitive in a world without controls and with increased competition.

Initially, companies responded by merging with or acquiring companies in other markets. Some moved their production to areas with cheaper labor and land, but since the advent of the computer globalization has increasingly meant the transfer of knowledge around the world. Asia's emerging economies provided a ready source of well-educated, cheap labor, and organizations and enterprises began to source their knowledge-workers overseas.

With the advent of the Internet, the effect of globalization on e-training and development has taken a further leap forward. It is no longer necessary for an organization's knowledge asset to be located in one place or one country. At the outset of the Internet boom, computer whiz-kids from Bangalore, India, were being wooed by Silicon Valley to help with business start-ups and be the backbone of the technology. Now those high-tech knowledge-workers can stay at home, very often literally, and be equally valuable to a parent organization a continent away.

THE STAGES OF EVOLUTION

Today's e-trainers suggest that the industry's history began with the Internet, or perhaps a decade or so earlier with the advent of computer-based training. But the ideas behind people being able to learn at their own pace, using the latest technology to help them understand new ideas and concepts, is rather older than most "geeks" might like to think.

The timeline below charts the developments in the "industry" recording the key events.

TIME-LINE – THE EVOLUTION OF E-TRAINING AND DEVELOPMENT

» **AD 50–60:** St Paul writes his first epistle, full of doctrinal teaching. He chides his distant readers for errors, answers questions, and gives directions for conduct.

» **1837:** Using the recently introduced Penny Post, English phonographer Isaac Pitman teaches correspondence courses on shorthand in the UK. His brother, Ben Pitman, who founded the Phonographic Institute in Cincinnati, Ohio, to teach and publish work on shorthand, introduced Pitman's shorthand system to the US in 1852. Pitman shorthand has been adapted into 15 languages and is still one of the most used shorthand systems in the world.

» **1856:** Language Teaching by Correspondence introduced by Frenchman Charles Toussaint and German Gustav Langenscheidt, who organized a school in Berlin for language teaching by correspondence. This self-study teaching system used practical phonetic transcription. Students were offered opportunities to submit questions but not encouraged to do so.

» **1873:** In Boston, Massachusetts, Anna Ticknor establishes the Society to Encourage Studies at Home, to provide educational opportunities for women across class boundaries. Although largely a volunteer organization, over 10,000 members participated in its correspondence instruction over a 24-year period. Ticknor becomes known as the "mother of American correspondence study."

» **1883–1891:** The first official recognition of education by correspondence comes from Chautauqua College of Liberal Arts. This college was authorized by the State of New York to grant academic degrees to students who successfully completed work at the summer institutes and by correspondence during the academic year.

» **1892:** William Rainey Harper establishes the first college-level courses by mail at the University of Chicago, creating the world's first university distance-education program.

» **1910–1920:** Pitman introduces visual instruction, including lantern-slides and motion pictures being added to the repertory of many courses.

» **1918–40:** The first educational radio licenses are granted to the University of Salt Lake City, the University of Wisconsin, and the University of Minnesota. Pennsylvania State College broadcasts courses over the radio. The Federal Communications Commission granted educational radio broadcasting licenses to 202 colleges, universities, and school boards between 1918 and 1946. By 1923 over 10% of all broadcast radio stations were owned by educational institutions that delivered educational programming. By 1940 there was only one college-level credit course offered by radio and that course failed to attract any enrollments.

» **1922:** Thomas Edison predicts that motion pictures would replace textbooks, and perhaps teachers, in the classroom.

» **1933:** Televised courses offered by the State University of Iowa.
» **1964:** Funded by the Carnegie Corporation, the University of Wisconsin's Articulated Instructional Media (AIM) Project seeks ways to incorporate various communication media into instructional curricula. The idea tested by the AIM Project was that self-directed learners could benefit from the strengths of multiple modes of content presentation and interaction alternatives. The program used correspondence materials, study guides, radio and television broadcasts, audiotapes, and telephone-conferencing to provide instruction for "off-campus" students. The project demanded a systems approach to program development, and it demonstrated that the functions of a teacher could be divided between teams of specialists and then reintegrated to provide a total distance-learning program.
» **1967:** Britain's Open University founded. It is the largest and most innovative educational organization in the world and is a leader in the large-scale application of technology to facilitate distance learning. The success of the Open University was the major reason for the development of open universities in other countries, such as America and Japan. There are more than 218,000 people currently studying with the Open University.
» **1974:** John Bear publishes his first guide to education by non-traditional methods. It covers night and weekend colleges, foreign medical schools, degrees *via* the Internet and other e-mail avenues. The thirteenth edition, containing details of over 2000 programs, is out now.
» **1975:** Coast College, USA, buys 15 answering machines to record students' messages for telecourse instructors, who replied within 48 hours.
» **1982:** The National University Teleconferencing Network (NUTN) uses satellite broadcasting among 40 of its institution members.
» **1987:** Mind Extension University, a cable network broadcasting courses and full degree programs developed by community colleges and universities, is founded.

> » **1984–1993:** The multimedia computer-based training era – starting on mainframes, growth was slow until the advent of the PC.
> » **1991–1994:** Network applications (e-mail) makes its debut in the learning process.
> » **1994–2000:** The Internet is "born" and early web-based training programs are introduced. The Internet becomes the medium of choice for educators, but is still constrained by lack of bandwidth, meaning picture quality is limited and download time slow.
> » **2000–2004:** Technological advances, including JAVA/IP network applications, rich streaming-media, high-bandwidth access, and advanced Website design, revolutionize training methods. Live instructor-led training (ILT) via the Web can be combined with real-time mentoring, improved learner services, and up-to-date and fully engaging "born on the Web" content.
> » **2002–2006:** M-learning, using mobile phones, PDAs, and other delivery methods is introduced and becomes commonplace.

PROFITABILITY – THE ACID TEST

Despite the clear historical connection between all the technologies involved in the training and development process, few of today's key players in the industry have their pedigree in either the correspondence college or distance-learning organization sectors. However, the business models being used by the new generation of e-learning corporations would not be unfamiliar to them.

Coast Community College, California, using a provision of the US Higher Education Act, funded a two-year task force (1970–1972) to design the television course, or "telecourse," of the future. The project involved all California community and State colleges, along with the University of California. Working in 1972, the task force predicted many of the technological innovations that today we take for granted, including development of the digital compact disc.

The task force defined a telecourse as a complete course of study in a given subject, not adjunct curricula like a single movie, filmstrip, slide show, audiotape, or vinyl record. Students are separated from the teacher, standing or sitting before a camera in a classroom or studio somewhere else, in real time or not. Provisions must be made for such teaching functions as answering student questions, setting and grading tests, and reporting student progress to the school. All curricula must meet established academic standards.

The task force applied a relatively simple business model, not dissimilar to that being used by the current generation of e-learning corporations. Colleges and universities using the telecourse would pay a license fee to the telecourse distributor, which in turn paid telecourse producers, with copyright ownership to be negotiated.

Co-ordinating the development, distribution, and licensing of tele-courses was assigned to Coastline Community College, which arranged for classes with top instructors to be broadcast by public television station KOCE to colleges, universities, and libraries in Orange County. Having no physical campus, Coastline was the first "virtual college." By 1976, backed by grants from Kellogg and other corporations, Coastline was serving 18,500 students within a 150-square-mile area of southern California. It was also doing something that no other e-learning venture appeared to be doing – it was making money.

Brandon-Hall (see Chapter 9) runs a share-tracking service for the sector and as at June 2002 the portfolio looked sick. In 2001, the three providers of learning-management software with the most customers – Blackboard Inc., eCollege, and WebCT Inc. – predicted that they would be profitable some time in 2002, but they are not profitable yet. In the first quarter of 2002, Blackboard posted revenue of $14.7mn, 103% of the $7.3mn it earned in the same period last year and 5% more than in the fourth quarter of 2001.

For the first quarter of 2002, eCollege had revenue of $5.6mn, 33% more than in the same period last year. Some 85,000 students are enrolled in courses that use the company's technology, almost 50% more than last year. WebCT's revenue for 2001 was 292% of its 2000 revenue, and its customer base increased by 750 institutions, or 40%, over the same period. The company now serves more than 2500 institutions in 81 countries.

But despite all the activity, no one is making serious money yet. The 23 e-learning companies with publicly-traded shares were worth nearly 24% less than at the same time two years ago, at a time when the NASDAQ index was down only 5% on the same period.

The problem seems to stem from where the new e-learning companies came from. With names like Click2Learn, Learn2.com, Skillsoft, and SmartForce, it's not hard to recognize these as businesses from the dot.com era. The Internet is undoubtedly the fastest-growing market in the history of the world. Its strengths in content, communication, and collaboration are, no doubt, ideally suited to learning and education applications. The emergence of the Internet as a distribution channel and the development of Web-based business models in the education industry have created a new competitive landscape. But like much of the rest of the dot.com sector, profits have proved elusive. Until they become profitable, the evolution process for the industry can be seen as still being at a formative stage.

NOTES

1 Worldwide and US Corporate IT Education and Training Services – Forecast Analysis, 1999–2004. IDC (2000).

2 The American Society for Training & Development International Comparisons Report.

3 Ferris, G.R. (1999) "Human Resource Management – Some New Directions." *Journal of Management*, May–June.

4 Witzel, M. (2000) *Human Resources Management*. Thoemmes Press, Bristol.

5 Cortada, J. (1998) *Rise of the Knowledge Worker*, pp. 72–9. Butterworth-Heinemann, Woburn, Massachusetts.

6 Kilco, W. & Munson, K. (2000) "E-Learning – Revolution or Evolution?" *e-learning*, May, pp. 3–12.

The E-Dimension

The Internet and organizational intranets open up a wealth of new learning opportunities that impact on every aspect of society. This chapter considers:

» how e-training and development is viewed from the perspectives of: the economy; the organization; the team; and the individual;
» the effect on lifelong learning;
» tracking – training's missing link;
» making e-training and development successful; and
» best practice – US West.

The Internet and organizational intranets have opened up a wealth of new learning opportunities that impact on every aspect of society, and this chapter considers e-training and development from different perspectives within that dimension.

THE ECONOMY

Even the most successful economies feel that they are being left behind in the race to improve the living standards and opportunities for their citizens. This is what the Conference Board of Canada has to say about its expectations of e-training and development:[1]

"Despite a high standard of living, Canada is falling behind other countries because of its relatively poor innovation and productivity performance. E-learning is one answer to sweeping global changes and our own labor market and productivity issues. E-learning affords small and medium-sized enterprises (SMEs), as well as large organizations, an opportunity to provide workplace learning, and it gives Canada a chance to close its 'digital divide' through the development of e-literacy.

"E-learning is being spurred on in Canada by three broad drivers:

» the global economic context;
» the human capital context; and
» the information and communications technology context.

"E-learning can be viewed as a means of delivering three key outcomes: improved and consistent rates of lifelong learning, improved productivity and improved innovation and competitiveness. Another desired outcome is increased equity. The issue of equity raises questions that need to be addressed now. Do Canadians currently have access to these learning technologies, is access to e-learning equally distributed by income, age and educational levels, and are barriers to e-learning such as cost and lack of information, time and content, being addressed? E-learning, like all learning, should yield outcomes that benefit society and the economy.

"As Statistics, Canada's most recent Adult Education and Training Survey report, notes: It is not enough, though, to look only at economic factors – income, employability and firm productivity … market payoffs of higher wages or employment. It is now well documented that learning leads to better health and other favorable outcomes for family, community and country.[2]

"Knowledge is a key determinant of sustained economic growth because knowledge, unlike other factors of production, is not subject to diminishing returns."[3]

THE ORGANIZATION

E-training and development provides organizations with an unprecedented opportunity. The information and communications technologies that characterize our age are redefining the future of learning in the workplace. Organizations can use e-training and development to advance the knowledge and skills of their employees and to create lifelong learners. Now organizations can assess employees' learning needs, update content on a regular basis to fulfill those needs, track and recognize employees' learning, and deliver it at work or at home through exciting e-training and development applications. Organizations are most interested in the potential of e-training and development for just-in-time, modular learning. By leveraging workplace technologies, e-training and development can bridge the gap that has traditionally separated learning from work. Learning can be integrated into work more effectively because employees will use the same tools and technology for learning as they use for work. Both organizations and employees recognize that e-training and development will diminish the narrowing gap between work and home, and between work and learning.

The use of technology for learning transcends all types of work – it encompasses the shop floors of the "old economy" as much as the cubicles of the "new economy." In fact, lifelong learning and workplace education are as essential to competitiveness as both types of economies are. E-training and development is an option for any organization looking to improve the skills and capacity of its employees.

Employers have identified three main reasons to use e-training and development:[4]

1 **Just-in-time learning** – employers can integrate individual learning with individual needs and provide employees with the knowledge

and skills when they need them. Employees don't have to take whole courses. They can just take the "modules" of learning that fit their current needs.

2 **Cost-effectiveness** – significant savings come from reduced travel expenses and reduced venue costs, and lost productivity time is less as employees can spend "down-time" in training. IBM, for example, is reported as having avoided more than $80mn in travel and housing expenses in 1999 by deploying online learning across its worldwide operations.

3 **Improved employee morale** – staff are better motivated by being able to retain some of the initiative in training matters. For example, the "one size fits all" philosophy of classroom and instructor-based training has been replaced by tailor-made programs. Online courses can pre-test trainees to ascertain their level of knowledge and then adapt the course structure and content to their needs, reducing time wasted in covering old ground.

In a recent study of the 29 most advanced economies in the world, the OECD also found the key benefits of e-learning to be reduced cost and increased flexibility.[5]

A further major benefit to organizations comes from the discipline that online learning forces onto organizations in the way they manage the information raw material that is used to support training online. Many corporate intranets have thousands of pages posted in a haphazard manner. Current important information sits alongside irrelevant out-of-date pages and no one can easily tell the difference between them.

Having a knowledge structure is a vital component of the e-training process. It is a vital tool in keeping thousands of employees spread across continents and time zones constantly informed about changes in products, prices, terms of trade, and competitors.

BEST PRACTICE – US WEST INC.

US West, the Denver-based 120-year-old telecom giant that serves 14 US states and 25 million customers, found itself facing a major challenge in 1999. Despite having leadership in Digital

Subscriber Line (DSL) services, advanced frame-relay, the country's largest Web-based yellow pages, PCS wireless, and a network that featured more than 99% digital switching, they were having trouble keeping their customer services representatives on top of all the changes in products, promotions, pricing, and, of course, all the information coming in on their competitors. As if this was not enough, they had to sharpen their sales skills and keep a close watch on customer satisfaction levels. They also needed to work with their front-line staff to ensure that as well as being well-trained they knew how to respond to customers' current needs and problems.

Relying on printed documents, sales briefings, and training sessions did not ensure cross-company accuracy or that the information reached everyone who needed it. US West had online procedures databases but each document looked different and content was up to the individual authors who had their own views as to what was important.

In 1999, InfoBuddy, US West's intranet-based knowledge management system replaced the old systems, and, as well as customer service, supported a wide variety of job functions, such as technical repair, installation, and maintenance. InfoBuddy is a methods and procedures database with intelligent knowledge-management capabilities, such as searching, tagging, and a customizable interface. It is capable of reorganizing the presented information for different users dependent on their job function or role, experience, qualification, or any other predetermined criteria. Each user can also personalize the system using the "MyBuddy" feature. The system is both reactive and proactive. It "sends" information on, for example, new promotions, pricing policies, and so forth, to the computer desktops of those involved in the program.

US West achieved enormous efficiencies using InfoBuddy over its old learning systems. Customer representatives are trained and developed in a more cost-effective and timely manner, using a system that allows the company to grow and change its structure to meet the fast-changing nature of the market it serves.

TEAMS

Since the 1980s there has been considerable emphasis on team development, led by Professor Meredith Belbin, who identified and explained the roles and drivers of team performance.[6] Until the advent of e-learning systems, little practical recognition was taken of a team's training needs, except using systems that reinforced the inflexibility of team structures. Teams were, and in many cases still are, trained in the same way at the same time. This is debilitating for the organization when a whole section of people is missing for a training period. It also assumes everyone in the team has much the same needs.

The reality of teams today is that their memberships are geographically disparate and, as people stay in one organization for less time than they once did, their training and development needs are rarely identical. Yet in the traditional training environment they are often put on the same course on the same subject and in one country or location.

Some of the methods of online training and development of particular benefit to teams include the following.

» **Discussion rooms** – usually facilitated by a trainer, these on-screen areas allow people to exchange ideas on relevant topics. They can be a rich source of new and innovative ideas, along the lines of brainstorming sessions. But in this respect they have the added advantage of not being conducted in a classroom, in that less pushy participants can have their say too. Discussion rooms can take place in real-time and can include videoconferencing, or they can take the form of a "notice board," with discussions posted at convenient times. This can make it easier for people in different time zones to take part.
» **Online briefings** – these enable each person to receive the same information from the trainer facilitating the event as every other team member. But although all participants receive the information at the same time, they don't have to act on it straight away. They can either wait until their work pattern allows them to focus on it or until they actually need to apply the knowledge concerned. As one telesales support manager put it: "It's very quiet at work right now. All our key customers are away at a national conference for the day. Things will pick up fast tonight or tomorrow morning, but right now I am

catching up on a training program I'm doing online to get a better handle on some new products we are about to launch."

» **Conferencing** - whether by telephone or video systems, conferencing *via* a computer and the Internet is a powerful way to train teams without too much travel time being involved. It's about as close as you can get to being in the same room and has one benefit not always easily obtained elsewhere: you can let those team members who are unable to attend see an action replay at their convenience, or the session can be reviewed later to gain additional learning points.

THE INDIVIDUAL

The Conference Board of Canada study referred to above came up with the list of factors, in Table 4.1 below, that employees believe are important to them. This seems to suggest that, whilst they recognize the value of learning technologies, they don't always see them as being the best or only way to train. Providers of e-training material have not been slow to recognize this and have come up with their own suitably jargonistic title - "blended learning" (see Chapter 6).

The key benefits of these findings may be summarized as follows.

» **Self-paced tuition** - people can work as quickly or as slowly as their own particular circumstances permit.

Table 4.1 Conference Board of Canada study on learning technologies.

Learning Technologies	Yes	No	Sometimes
Can be used any time	73	5	22
Convenient	73	0	27
Provides me with relevant learning	68	0	32
Gives me control over learning	66	0	34
Supported by management	64	5	31
An effective way to learn workplace knowledge and skills	62	2	36
Easy to use	46	3	51
Encourages learning in groups	20	49	31
The best way to learn	12	7	81

» **Convenient learning** – people can set aside time when they can choose to access the information and focus on it.

» **Quick responses** – turnaround of queries and feedback on submitted work is much faster via the Internet than by normal mail channels, especially when people are working at remote sites.

» **E-delivery of assignments** – where a learner has to provide pieces of work such as exam papers, assignments, or projects, these can be submitted electronically, cutting down on administration and being delivered instantaneously. Feedback and marks can be sent back in the same way, thus allowing any errors or misunderstandings to be put right quickly.

» **Being part of a learning team** – learning networks can be a very effective way of sharing knowledge and experiences.

» **Access to all relevant information** – each individual has access to a wealth of information provided by the organization, either *via* an intranet (see US West case) or via the Internet.

» **Tutor support and help-lines** – learners can seek advice from their tutors or trainers on a one-to-one basis. This can be a very important aspect of any development program. Although a telephone conversation with a trainer is more personal and can offer a speedy solution, the e-mail approach has a number of distinct advantages. For example, it allows the trainer to:
  » consider each response more carefully;
  » carry out further research if a question demands it; and
  » send any advice of a general nature to other learners in the program.

» **Stimulates and encourages lifelong learning** – with a 40–60% reduction in costs compared with classroom learning,[7] individuals will have less difficulty in taking long-term learning projects with them to new jobs, where either the new employer will feel comfortable with the relatively modest cost or the employees themselves can foot the bill without too much pain.

TRACKING – TRAINING'S MISSING LINK

To get the best out of any training and development program the following basic rules need to be followed.

1 Introduce a routine that ensures all employees attending training are briefed at least a week beforehand on what to expect and what is expected of them.

2 Ensure that all employees discuss with their manager or supervisor what they got out of the training program – in particular, whether it met the expectations of both. This should take place no later than a week after the program.

3 Check within a month (or another appropriate time period) and then again at regular intervals to see whether skills have been improved, and that those skills are being put into practice.

4 Evaluate the costs and financial benefits of your training and development plans, and use this information to help set the next training budget.

Most organizations are poor at delivering against these tasks. The training gets done, but rarely is there any follow-up analysis. The great strength of e-systems in training and development is that they provide an automatic "audit trail" of everything you could possibly need to know about the training program event and its outcomes.

Unlike manual, paper-based programs that depend on trainers documenting events, once set up, an e-training program can prompt all the participants to respond to questions, consolidate the results, and produce reports on outcomes.

NOTES

1 Conference Board of Canada (2001) "E-Learning for the Workplace – Creating Canada's Lifelong Learners," p. 3.

2 Bérubé, G., Salmon, W., & Tuijnman, A. (2001) "A Report on Adult Education and Training in Canada – Learning a Living," 81-586-XIE (Ottawa: Statistics Canada and Human Resources Development Canada), p. 5.

3 Applied Research Branch, Strategic Policy, Human Resources Development Canada, (1996) "Technological and Organizational Change and Labor Demand – the Canadian Situation," R-97-1E, Ottawa.

4 Conference Board of Canada (2001) "Employers Ramp Up With E-Learning," pp. 9–13. The results are an aggregate of organizations with a mean size of 600 employees. The sample of 830 organizations

was pulled from a universe consisting of 6827 Canadian organizations having 100 employees or more, proportionately representing Canada's population.

5 OECD, Education Policy Analysis (1999 edition), p. 25.
6 Belbin, M. (1981) *Why They Succeed or Fail*. Butterworth-Heinemann, Oxford.
7 Towner, N. (2001) "Remote Control." *e-business review*, June, p. 36.

The Global Dimension

- » Global e-laws rule, OK?
- » Power to the global knowledge-worker.
- » Breaking the language barrier.
- » World standards for a global economy.

"If you really want to know where things are going in e-learning, you have to look five to eight years out. And looking five to eight years from now, a number of things are already clear.

"First, the underlying technological change driving this revolution is mind-numbingly predictable. This may seem odd given the unpredictability of technology in the financial markets. For example, we can't predict what Nortel's stock price will look like in six months, let only six weeks from now.

"But the underlying technical drivers here are entirely predictable because they are an accumulation of scientific wisdom and breakthrough research that is 30 or 40 years old."

David Pecaut, president of iFormation Group, based on remarks to the Learning Partnership, Toronto, June 7, 2001

THE GLOBAL E-LAWS

What David Pecaut had in mind, and expanded on in his remarks when he talked about predictability, was what have come to be widely regarded as the immutable laws of technology and the Internet. The effects of these laws on the globalization of e-knowledge are perhaps the most profound drivers in this field.

The first of these is Moore's Law, named after Gordon Moore, co-founder of Intel, who suggested that every 24 months, computing capacity would fall by half in cost. He coined this law in the 1960s and it has since been updated to state that computer capacity will halve in cost every 18 months. Another way of looking at this is to say that for every dollar spent, you will be able to buy twice as much computing capacity 18 months from now. An example of Moore's Law is that all the computing power that was used by NASA in getting a man on the moon 40 years ago is now sitting in the homes of everyone with a computer capable of playing an averagely sophisticated computer game. This law in turn means that learners in even the poorest parts of the global economy have, or will shortly have, access to e-training programs of mind-blowing complexity. Ironically, in some parts of Africa the biggest barrier is the supply of electricity and not lack of computer capacity. Producing clockwork power-supplies with solar ancillary systems is solving this problem – all that users need is muscle power and a good supply of sunlight to get into e-learning mode.

The second law, referred to as Gilder's Law, has to do with the cost of transmitting information. Named after US technology business commentator George Gilder, it states that every nine months, the amount of information you can transmit doubles; or, nine months down the road, a given amount of information can be transmitted for half of the cost. This rate, as with Moore's Law, is accelerating because of the aggressive growth of other technologies, in this case fiber-optics and the ability to manage digital information through optical networking.

To illustrate Gilder's Law, if you were to take the entire contents of the British Library in London and send it to Cape Town, South Africa, it would take about 35 minutes and could cost as little as €1. This means that a company in Glasgow, Scotland, could be doing business with a company in Bangalore, India, and be completely indifferent as to how much data it is sending, or what it costs. For them, it would be essentially free. In 10 years, telecoms for most companies will be almost a free commodity.

The third law is Metcalfe's Law, named after Robert Metcalfe, who founded 3Com Corporation and designed the Ethernet protocol for computer networks. He came up with the notion that a network is only valuable when you add people to it. This may seem obvious, but what he went on to hypothesize was that the usefulness of a network equals the square of the number of users. So, if you've got 10 people in the network and you add another 10, the value has not doubled, but has increased tenfold. This is not unlike what happened with the telephone half a century ago. As costs came down and people realized their networking value, everyone wanted to have one in their home. It took nearly 50 years to reach 90% coverage of the developed world. The mobile phone has taken barely a decade to reach a similar saturation level. The economics of Metcalfe's Law mean that by 2010, 95% of the population of the developed world, including much of Asia, will be able to be on the Internet 24 hours a day, whenever they choose to be. Ten years from now, with long-distance communication essentially free, computing power enormous, and Internet users connected all the time, e-training and development programs will have the same global reach as oxygen has in the world's atmosphere.

The fourth law is perhaps not so much a law as the destruction of an old law brought about by the advent of the other three laws. Until the

Internet, there was a fundamental trade-off between two very different ways of communicating and teaching. The first method is typified at its pinnacle by Oxford and Cambridge Universities' one-to-one tutorial system – here the best teachers in the world and the student are in what can be best described as a "learning rich" environment. The subject can be tailored precisely to a particular student's needs, the pace of learning set appropriately, and there is the facility to ask questions and ponder answers. The second method is concerned with getting to as many students as possible, using what could perhaps best be described as "average" teachers. In this way of communication "richness" is traded for "reach" and until 1994 that law had proved immutable.

The Internet breaks the trade-off between richness and reach. A wide bandwidth, free communications, and the power of Moore's Law mean that it is now possible to have enormous richness, huge simulation power, and the ability for interactivity *and* enormous reach.

The possibilities for global education are boundless. Education has been limited by traditional ways of thinking about and delivering learning, which made richness and reach mutually exclusive. Educators are only now waking up to the challenges and prospects that will be brought by having the right technology to reach the whole world (see Fig. 5.1).

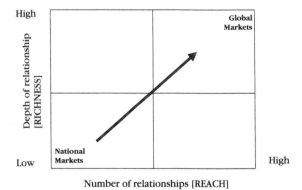

Fig. 5.1 Globalization of e-training and development.

Globalization, and the communications technologies that in part are driving that phenomenon, is making possible new networks that bring benefits to both learners and practitioners alike. The British Association for Open Learning (BAOL), a network of over 200 member organizations from across the education and learning sectors in the UK, now receives more enquiries from overseas, *via* the Internet, than from within the UK. It has begun to sign-up new members from across the globe, which brings an added dimension to its already active online discussion groups.

The MIT case study below shows that the richness of access to the best teaching brains in the world is now within the reach of everyone on the planet who has access to a $700 computer and a phone line.

THE MIT CASE STUDY

At a press conference on April 4, 2001, MIT (Massachusetts Institute of Technology) announced its commitment to make the materials from virtually all of its courses freely available on the World Wide Web for non-commercial use. This new initiative, called MIT OpenCourse-Ware (OCW) reflects MIT's institutional commitment to disseminate knowledge across the globe.

MIT sees OCW as a way to share its thinking about the content of a modern curriculum in all the areas in which it excels. Users of the OCW site may include other academics around the world and individual learners who may not have access to similar educational materials.

The task of creating a highly visible Website that draws together the materials of virtually all of MIT's course offerings is considerable. However, the majority of the faculty support this effort and believe that it is consistent with MIT's longstanding objective to focus the contributions of both its faculty and its new technologies on broad societal benefits.

The idea behind OCW is to make available on the web MIT course materials that are used in the teaching of almost all undergraduate and graduate subjects, free of charge to any user anywhere in the world. OCW will radically alter technology-enhanced education at MIT, and will serve as a model for university dissemination of knowledge in the Internet age. Such a venture will continue the tradition at MIT (and in American higher education) of open dissemination of educational materials, philosophy, and modes of thought, and will help lead to fundamental changes in the way colleges and universities engage the Web as a vehicle for education.

OCW will make available the core teaching materials that are used in MIT classes. Depending on the particular class or the style in which the course is taught, this could include material such as lecture notes, course outlines, reading lists, and assignments for each course. More technically sophisticated content will be encouraged.

The materials on the OCW site will be open and freely available worldwide for non-commercial purposes such as research and education, providing an extraordinary resource which others can adapt to their own needs. Faculty at colleges and universities around the world can use the OCW materials to develop new curricula and specific courses. These materials might be of particular value in developing countries that are trying to expand their higher education systems rapidly. Individual learners could draw upon the materials for self-study or supplementary use.

Other experiments in educational technology at MIT include:

» **The TEAL Project** – this will establish a technology-enabled active learning (TEAL) environment for large-enrollment physics courses, which will serve as a national model for such instruction. Building on the experience of other universities, TEAL will merge lectures, recitations, and hands-on laboratory experience into a technologically and collaboratively rich experience. Software and teaching materials developed in this effort will be made available nationally at little or no cost, in the hope of motivating a national effort along these lines.

» **I-Lab** – the goal of this is to provide online access to a remote laboratory for classes which, due to cost, space, and other reasons, do not include an on-site laboratory, and to deliver the educational benefits of hands-on experimentation to students anywhere, at any time.

» **The ArchNet Project** – this is based on the idea that educational technology should be employed to create and enhance learning communities. All community members will have individual workspaces in ArchNet which provide them with personalized entry points to the system, and which also allow them to represent themselves and their work to other members of the community. Learning community environments of this sort will be very widely used in professional education in the coming years.

MIT is also engaged in several collaborative and distance-learning projects around the world. In the future the technologies that are being developed to support these efforts will also be utilized to enhance OCW materials. Some of these projects include a policy on intellectual property ownership – the approach to the intellectual property created for MIT OCW will be clear and consistent with other policies for scholarly material used in education. Faculty will retain ownership of most materials prepared for MIT OCW, following the MIT policy on textbook authorship. MIT will retain ownership only when significant use has been made of its resources, so if student coursework is placed on the MIT OCW Website, then copyright in the work remains with the student.

The Andrew W. Mellon Foundation and the William & Flora Hewlett Foundation jointly provided the initial $11mn funding for the first 27 months of MIT OCW. They anticipate that development costs over a 10-year period will be between $7.5mn and $10mn per year.

POWER TO THE GLOBAL KNOWLEDGE-WORKER

Paul Stacey,[1] director of Corporate Education and Training at the Technical University of British Columbia, Canada, a long-time professional in e-teaching research, demonstrates that the knowledge-based economy puts a premium on intellectual capital. To develop that capital, particularly in high-tech, knowledge and skills must be continually updated and enhanced. High-tech workers know that their marketability is based on the currency of their skills, and jump from one company to the next for a chance to work on challenging, leading-edge projects. Increasingly, potential hires are asking in the interview not just about leading-edge work but how the company supports professional development. The heightened competition for skilled human resources is causing organizations to look closely at how recruitment and retention practices affect their intellectual capital and competitive position.

In the midst of all this, e-learning is emerging as a key enabler. For companies, e-learning provides a means for aligning workplace performance with business strategies and for building communities of best practice and expert thinking. For high-tech professionals, e-learning provides a new form of professional development that can provide up-to-date knowledge in small incremental units that fit around increasingly time-constrained lives, whilst enhancing their value in an increasingly global market for trained people.

According to the UNDP Human Development Report,[2] "more than half of the GDP of the major OECD countries is now knowledge-based," which in turn will increase the importance of the role of e-training and development in the global context.

BREAKING THE LANGUAGE BARRIER

Dawn Gareiss,[3] in a recent paper, cited the example of Litton PRC, an IT consulting and systems-integration subsidiary of Litton Industries Inc., which has a global e-learning program that trains 5400 employees in 80 offices, across 16 time zones worldwide. What started six years ago with 150 technology courses on CD-ROMs now comprises 1500 online courses on everything from interpersonal skills to Java. There's even 24-hour access to online mentors.

The most obvious challenges for any global e-learning implementation are language and localization issues. Many companies offer courses only in English, or in English and one other language, usually Spanish. Companies that want to offer courses in several languages usually turn to translators. Financial services provider GE Capital relies on translation companies to offer Web-based courses in English, French, German, and Japanese. But it's not enough just to convert a course from one language to another. "Globalness," to use Gareiss's term, requires localization or ways to ensure the learning makes sense in a local context. For example, the translation company may not be up to speed on GE language, so they have GE employees fluent in each local language review the translation to make sure it's GE-correct.

For example, as part of an e-business course that GE Capital offers, students had to visit specific Websites, but the assigned sites were from the US and appropriate only for English-speaking students. To make the course more relevant for other students, localization experts identified Websites in various languages that were just as useful.

Cisco sets the standard for the rest of the industry – it has a centralized pool of courses customized for specific regions of the world and individual students. The Cisco Networking Academy Program trains hundreds of thousands of high-school and college students around the world, offering courses in 11 languages via software from Lionbridge Technologies Inc. The LionAccess module lets Cisco upload and download files for translation; LionPath routes new and changed files; LionLinguist lets Cisco leverage previous translations; and LionView is a portal that Cisco managers can use to track globalization projects.

WORLD STANDARDS FOR A GLOBAL ECONOMY

One of the challenges that e-learning can help organizations surmount is ensuring that training and development are available so that employees can reach the same high standard in whichever country they are working. Cisco's e-training and development programs achieve this goal. Many other organizations – from high-tech firms such as Microsoft and Oracle, through safety-critical firms such as Qantas and British Airways, and global household names such as McDonald's – all have to hit a common corporate standard, albeit for different reasons.

At McDonald's Hamburger University,[4] McDonalds employees from Toledo to Taipei have begun attending Web-based classes to learn proper etiquette for greeting customers and the finer points of food assembly. Counter staff at Thrifty Car Rental franchises in close to 60 countries are logging on to the Web to brush up on their fleets and their insurance plans. Neptune Orient Lines (NOL), a 152-year-old, $2.3bn global container transportation company, is training its 12,000 employees based everywhere from the larger cities in Europe to the hinterlands of China, India, Bangladesh, or South America.

E-learning systems allow this to be done with comparative ease, compared with the procedures available for standardizing training and development programs in the pre-Internet era. Deloitte and Kodak[5] are just some of the companies that have benefited from the use of e-training and development to set and maintain common standards across their global markets.

NOTES

1 Stacey, P. (2000) "The Knowledge-Based Economy." *E-Learning*, May 26, pp. 3–4.
2 UNDP Human Development Report Office (1999), Human Development Report.
3 Gareiss, D. (2001) "E-Learning Around the World." *Information-week.com*, February 26.
4 Hall, Brandon (2001) "Taking Learning to Every Corner of the World." brandonhall.com.
5 Vaas, L. (2001) "The E-Training of America." *eWeek*, December 26.

The State of the Art

- » The foundations of e-training and development.
- » The e-training and development value chain and market map.
- » E-learning infrastructures.
- » Who uses e-training?
- » Subjects addressed by e-trainers.
- » The next stages of development.

THE FOUNDATIONS OF E-TRAINING AND DEVELOPMENT

The basic concept of e-training and development is that instructors and students are separated by time, location, or both, and greater efficiencies can thereby be achieved (see Fig. 6.1).

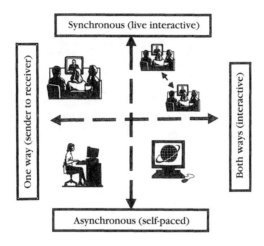

Fig. 6.1 The foundations of e-training and development.

Asynchronous training is e-learning in the more traditional sense. It involves self-paced learning – e.g. CDROM-based, network-based, intranet-based, or Internet-based. It may include access to instructors through online bulletin boards, online discussion groups, and e-mail, or it may be totally self-contained with links to reference materials instead of a ''live'' instructor.

Synchronous training is done in real time with a live instructor facilitating the training. Trainees log in at a set time and can communicate directly with the instructor and with each other. Trainees can ask questions and even view a whiteboard in much the same way as they would in a conventional classroom. Training lasts for a set amount of time – from a single session of 10 minutes upwards to several weeks, months, or even years. This type of training usually takes place *via* Websites, audio/videoconferencing, Internet telephony, or even two-way live broadcasts to students in a classroom.

Online support can be available to underpin both synchronous and asynchronous training methods. Online support comes in the form of forums, chat rooms, online bulletin boards, e-mail, live instant-messaging support, and knowledge databases offering indexed explanations and guidance. Online support offers the opportunity for more specific questions and answers, as well as more immediate answers.

THE E-TRAINING AND DEVELOPMENT VALUE CHAIN AND MARKET MAP

The e-training and development marketplace is large. Throughout the world, thousands of companies are providing products and services. One of the challenges everyone faces, sellers and buyers alike, is having a mental map of the market and an understanding of how different companies and organizations are positioned in it.

Paul Stacey[1] has created a simple and straightforward e-learning value chain and market map (Fig. 6.2), which explains the sector clearly.

Content in the e-training and development arena is made up of learning objects, units, modules, lessons, courses, programs, and – in the case of universities, both corporate and State, and colleges – entire curricula. E-learning content can be for credit or non-credit leading to certification, certificates, and degrees.

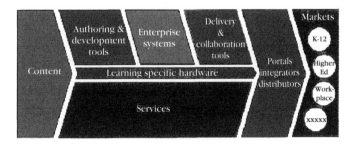

Fig. 6.2   E-learning value chain and market map.

E-training content can come from three main sources. It can be custom-developed for a particular user. This is the route favored by big business and the academic education market. Alternatively, it can be bought off-the-shelf in much the same way as paper-based training programs or indeed as most popular forms of computer software are bought. This is the way that most small firms and organizations in developing economies are most likely to go. A third alternative is to purchase off-the-shelf content and customize it to suit your organization and its needs.

The upper spur in the map depicts the technologies involved under the following three main headings.

» **Authoring and development tools** – these are used to create e-training content. There is a wide range of options available for authoring and developing e-learning content, including software applications for:
  » multimedia creation;
  » audio and video capture and edit;
  » design;
  » authoring HTML and XML;
  » developing Flash animations; and
  » Java programming.
» **Enterprise systems** – these are applications that are usually central-ized and set up for the whole organization. They are the applications that manage the e-training and development process from devel-opment to delivery. Software infrastructures here include Learning Management Systems, Learning Content Management Systems, and Knowledge Management Systems, which are examined in more detail below.
» **Delivery and collaboration tools** – these include applications for course delivery, live learning, collaboration, threaded discussion, sharing applications, and doing things like audio or video over IP. With the maturing of the e-learning marketplace technology, vendors are merging and acquiring each other. As a result, some vendors now have integrated tools and applications from each of the technology sectors, creating an integrated all-in-one system. Applications like WebCT or Blackboard, for example, offer elements of authoring,

learning management, and delivery. There is, according to Stacey, "a rapid blurring between the sectors."

The middle portion of Stacey's map is a small sector for learning-specific hardware. Inherent in e-learning is the need for computers and networks. However, there are really very few learning-specific hardware components on the market. Traditionally, e-learning hardware architectures have been client/server. Some vendors are now installing their e-learning on specifically configured hardware for ease of adoption and performance. Peer-to-peer e-learning and mobile e-learning *via* mobile phones and PDAs are beginning to make their presence felt (a subject that will be covered later in this chapter).

The bottom of the map shows the services sector. This is a big sector and there are numerous services on offer – everything from consulting on strategy and deployment to technical support, from planning e-learning to implementing pilots, to assessing results and scaling up.

Content, technology, and services all lead to eventual distribution to markets *via* the distributors and integrators sector. Learning portals also offer e-learners or organizations consolidated access to learning and training resources from multiple sources, *via* Websites. Operators of learning portals are also called content aggregators, distributors, or hosts.

The far right-hand side of the map shows e-learning markets. Primary e-learning markets are schools ("K-12" in US nomenclature), higher education, workplace, and consumers. Each market sector has different needs and requirements.

A recent study by Corporate University Xchange[2] revealed the scope of these different infrastructures for a number of key business sectors. Their study took in 65 organizations, ranging from those having robust e-learning systems to those providing e-learners with a gateway through an intranet site, to libraries of e-learning courseware supplied by vendors, such as SmartForce and Click2Learn.

E-LEARNING INFRASTRUCTURES

Figure 6.3 illustrates the major e-learning infrastructures currently being utilized by corporate learning organizations.

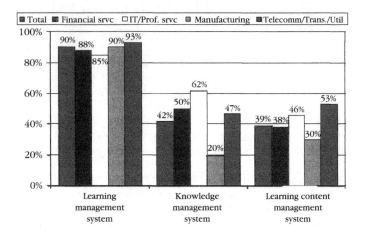

Fig. 6.3 E-learning infrastructures.

Learning management systems (LMS)

This is the most prolific group of software tools. Many started life as classroom booking tools, student records, multimedia database management tools, curriculum management tools, or online learning catalogs. Web-based technology makes it easy to integrate all this functionality. Ninety per cent of the corporate learning practitioners indicated they had a learning management system integrated into their overall e-learning architecture.

Whatever the origins of a typical LMS, they are all beginning to have the same features. A poll of 20 companies conducted in May, 2001 showed LMS functionality was attractive for e-learning but not for face-to-face events.[3] Companies seem attracted to the online learning monitoring feature of management systems. Student progress and progression to competency can be recorded.

Knowledge management systems (KMS)

These involves capturing, organizing, and storing knowledge and experiences of individual workers and groups within an organization and making it available to others in the organization. The information is stored in a special database called a knowledge base.

Training and development has changed from being a one-time event to more of a process. Learning is being incorporated into all stages of an individual's career and the distinctions between formal and informal learning and between training and performance support are blurring.

Based on these changes, many best practice organizations have realized the great potential in converging knowledge management systems with e-learning systems. Both systems share the common goal of diffusing knowledge throughout an entire organization. Cap Gemini Ernst & Young, First Consulting Group, and Level 3 Communications are examples of the many organizations that have taken on this effort.

According to the Corporate University Xchange's study, knowledge management systems were common among organizations that launched their learning initiative three to five years ago (57%), organizations that offer more than 100 courses (55%), and organizations that have invested more than 30% of their overall education/training budget in e-learning. IT and professional services organizations were also trendsetters in this area, with over 60% indicating that their e-learning infrastructure contained a knowledge management system.

Learning content management systems (LCMS)

These are software applications that allow trainers and training directors to manage both the administrative and content-related functions of training. The great attraction of LCMS is that they provide e-learning practitioners with a central repository for storing and managing their content. Nearly 40% of corporate learning practitioners indicated they had integrated LCMS into their overall e-learning architectures. LCMS allow organizations to provide their learners with just-enough and just-in-time information, as well as to create customized learning experiences based on their learners' needs. In addition, organizations that have LCMS were more likely to custom develop their own e-learning content than those who simply have LMS.

LMS and LCMS really have two very different functions. It's unfortunate that both have such similar names, which only helps to confuse even more. The primary objective of LMS is to manage learners, keeping

Table 6.1 LMS and LCMS explained.

	LMS	LCMS
Primary target users	Training managers, instructors, administrators	Content developers, instructional designers, project managers
Provides primary management of...	Learners	Learning content
Management of classroom, instructor-led training	Yes (but not always)	No
Performance reporting of training results	Primary focus	Secondary focus
Learner collaboration	Yes	Yes
Keeping learner profile data	Yes	No
Sharing learner data with an ERP system	Yes	No
Event scheduling	Yes	No
Competency mapping – skill gap analysis	Yes	Yes (in some cases)
Content creation capabilities	No	Yes
Organizing reusable content	No	Yes
Creation of test questions and test administration	Yes (73% of all LMS tools have this capability)	Yes (92% of all LCMS tools have this capability)
Dynamic pre-testing and adaptive learning	No	Yes
Workflow tools to manage the content development process	No	Yes
Delivery of content by providing navigational controls and learner interface	No	Yes

track of their progress and performance across all types of training activities. By contrast, LCMS manage content or learning objects that are served up to the right learner at the right time. Understanding the difference can be very confusing because most LCMS also have built-in LMS functionality. Brandon Hall[4] offers a table (see Table 6.1) as a useful aid to clearing up the confusion between these all too similar sounding terms.

WHO USES E-TRAINING AND DEVELOPMENT?

With such a young industry, in truth no one knows with any certainty the size or breakdown of the sectors. But Sam Adkins,[5] researching on behalf of Brandon Hall, has made an attempt by consolidating the data from various interested parties, for the US at least. That data is shown in chart form in Fig. 6.4.

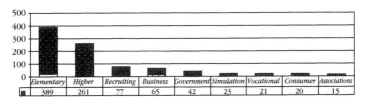

	Elementary	Higher	Recruiting	Business	Government	Simulation	Vocational	Consumer	Associations
■	389	261	77	65	42	23	21	20	15

Fig. 6.4 The US market for e-learning, 2002. Sources: brandonhall.com, US Department of Education, US Economic Census, American Staffing Association, Training and Simulation Association, American Society of Association Executives.

Wide adoption of e-training across all sectors is in evidence. However, the business sectors do not lead the field, despite the arguments surrounding the cost benefits of e-training versus conventional training methods. The academic sector is not only the largest, but is the fastest growing. The fact that children in schools and those in college and university education are being exposed to this subject now is reasonably indicative of a much wider level of general acceptance in the very near future, as they leave and take up employment.

SUBJECTS ADDRESSED BY E-TRAINERS

Peter Boulton[6] conducted a study to find out exactly what topics are currently being taught by e-trainers. The results are shown in Fig. 6.5.

The results show that, collectively, organizations are using e-training throughout most workplace topics – however, it is evident that the IT areas dominate the field. Management development is still very much a minority activity as far as e-learning is concerned. However the "other" section in this study included a fair mixture of organizations using e-learning tools to teach interpersonal and business/leadership skills development.

According to Stacey's research (referred to above), currently the most popular forms of e-learning content across the whole spectrum, including non-business organizations and individuals, include:

» technology;
» business;

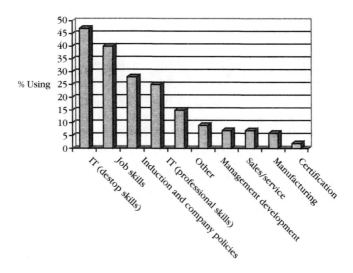

Fig. 6.5 Subjects addressed by e-trainers.

» social sciences;
» health and medicine;
» personal interest;
» education;
» science;
» vocational; and
» arts.

THE NEXT STAGES OF DEVELOPMENT

David Pecaut,[7] president of iFormation Group, in a talk to the Learning Partnership in Toronto on June 7, 2001, outlined what he saw as the four stages of adoption of e-learning, with the last two being very much in the future or, as he referred to them, "frontiers."

Stage 1

There is much evidence that most organizations, including probably most current users of e-training systems, are only at the beginning of the e-learning curve. Much of what is being used today is at the first point on the curve – "textware." It amounts to little more than taking a book, putting it online, and making it accessible on a 24/7 basis. This is hardly very innovative. It is simply taking existing material, applying old technology, and dumping it on the Web. Most college and school learners are using textware to get at more content more quickly, and businesses are coming into this arena too.

Stage 2

The next point on the e-learning curve is "software," which is where learners begin to have a more interactive experience online. This is what happens when pilots get trained on aircraft simulators, for instance. They could do hours and hours of one-to-one tutorials with someone telling them what it's like to fly a plane, but nothing compares to the power of sitting behind the controls of a 747 when the pilot has to face the consequences of what happens when he doesn't put the flaps down fast enough. In simulation, he'll feel it crash – blinding lights and the gravitational pull as he plunges to the ground.

Simulation offers a powerful way to learn because it requires decision making in real time. It also offers second and third chances to get it right. But learning software in the form of CDs is not the next frontier.

Stage 3

The next frontier is "humanware," and this is the frontier we're just getting to. It's a truer form of simulation that goes to the next level. It's the power to create, in an educational learning environment, the ability to foresee the kinds of decisions people will make, to respond to them in a way that feels intuitive and human, and then to provide them with clues to where the next cache of information lies.

There are companies at the forefront of this kind of training, for example Accenture, which has software that allows users to learn very complex tasks, like running a power plant or being able to service a piece of complex equipment, in real time. Users experience what it is to be a repair or salesperson, what it feels like to be the Air Canada pilot making decisions in real time. Being given additional information, and then being able to determine if those decisions are right or wrong, is what makes humanware a more advanced state of e-learning.

This near-reality experience not only improves learning, but it also boosts productivity. Companies that have implemented this kind of training find that the productivity – whether of a call-center worker, someone in a diagnostic role, a repair person, or even someone with a complex management job – improved dramatically, and by as much as 50–75% in some cases.

This training can take place with all kinds of human intervention behind it, and with costs falling dramatically, programs like this, which three years ago cost three to five million dollars, can now cost as little as $200,000 to create and deliver a full eight-hour course. So humanware is the third point on the e-learning curve, and it's one we're just starting to approach.

Stage 4

The fourth frontier is what Pecaut calls "everyware" and it is particularly relevant to e-learning. One of the problems in traditionally-delivered forms of education and training is that it happens in a classroom or a work setting at a specific time. You take exams at a certain time or you have to wait to use a computer at home to do your work.

Pecaut claims we're moving to a new point on the e-learning curve where we will have devices that allow us to be trained when and where we need to be trained. We will have the broadband capability to access our personal education program ourselves. We will also have the simulation capability to get both richness and reach. What's coming in the next five years is the ability to have the learning occur at any time, anywhere that we want, on hand-held devices.

Some of the most likely future developments are looked at below.

M-learning

The near ubiquitous mobile phone looks set to make an appearance on the e-training stage. However, to date the publicity around "mobile-everything," training included, has led to a considerable amount of frustration on the part of consumers. Whilst it is possible to access e-mail and surf the Internet on a mobile phone, service can be patchy, downloads painfully slow, and typing more than a sentence or two just plain hard work.

Equipment manufacturers have started to look into wireless solutions and are beginning to offer products that will eventually make ubiquitous computing a reality. But ideas here are still in their formative years. Elliott Masie, founder of the MASIE Center, an international e-lab and think-tank (see Chapter 9), warns that education may not be one of the earliest fields to benefit in a significant way from advances in mobile technology.

"A shift to a form factor is never going to happen because of learning," Masie claims.[8] "Learning follows function. We didn't start learning on PCs until we had PCs for a while; we're just now starting to learn on the net, after several years of experience. Nothing's really different about mobile learning. Inevitably, it will be used, but it will be a second, not first-wave utilization. We tend to take some time to get familiar with those things that are not mission critical. We play with our palmtop for a while before we start using it for critical business information."

Masie says the "first wave" of m-learning implementation is already beginning to take place on college and business campuses, where advanced wireless networks can be established, enabling users within a set geographic area to have high-speed wireless access to the Internet *via* palmtop devices and even mobile phones.

"Over time, we will find ways to make that level of wireless access a community standard," Masie says, "but it's not going to happen because of learning. It's going to happen because of other broadband desires [such as e-commerce]. The arrival of mobile learning in a full-fledged sense will happen six months to a year after mobile access is there for other applications."

Industry-watchers believe that effective voice-recognition technology will be the key to turning mobile phones into useful information devices. However, some workable m-learning innovations have already come onto the market.

Stanford University Law School is in the midst of a technology upgrade that will cost close to $10mn. A significant slice of that budget is going to set up a campus-wide, high-speed wireless network. Partnering with Cisco, Nokia, and Airwave – the latter a San Francisco Bay-area company providing high-speed wireless Internet services – Stanford has created a wireless system with 25 access points around the campus, where students can download to their laptops research, class assignments, and other information. Palm Inc. has added PalmPilots into the wireless mix, and working with other vendors – including PDA Verticals, NearSpace, Town Compass, and Elite.com – Stanford has come up with additional applications, including a mapping program to help navigate the Stanford campus, QuizApp, which helps students practice for exams, and a PeopleSoft application will allow students to register for classes wirelessly. Bluefish Wireless has installed access points around the law school, enabling students to not only download but also send files from their PalmPilots.

Peer-to-peer (P2P)

P2P isn't a training application – it's a networking technology that enables the sharing of resources. The "peers" are individual computers that make up the network. When a peer computer requests a resource, the network supplies the resource from another peer that happens to have it. The more distributed the resources, the more useful P2P networks become. Industry experts[9] believe this technology could have a big impact on the way people retrieve and act on information, as it has the potential to become the ultimate knowledge management system. The unmoderated environment lends itself to informal information exchange rather than formal training. As more peers join the network, opportunities for more information to be stored, accessed, exchanged, and used for learning are increased. P2P encourages a low level of collaboration between users. Learning comes into play when peers start to create communities of practice and make related content available across the network. The creation of shared spaces, such as those made available by Groove (www.groove.net), enables groups to collaborate over space and time, a key attribute of all e-training systems.

Organizations are already successfully using P2P as part of their training initiatives. Satellite Cops, a privately-owned company that sells and distributes satellite television and plasma displays, is using Groove to train its dispersed sales force. Satellite Cops introduced Groove over a year ago and it is used for training sales reps in satellite-TV sales, keeping them up-to-date on the latest promotions. Because they all work from home offices, they can push Web-pages or Word documents and discuss new projects – all while collaborating online. Before using Groove, Satellite Cops relied on a combination of e-mail, instant messaging, Web navigation, and telephone interaction to provide sales representatives with training materials, updated advertising and marketing materials, and presentations. Now all of those *ad hoc* interactions take place within a shared space, and any resulting data is saved within the project.

Blended learning

Blended learning combines the advantages of two learning methods – for example, classroom instruction and self-paced instruction delivered *via* the Internet. It seeks to capture the best of both worlds by allowing learners to pick and choose how they want to learn, and it affords them greater flexibility and convenience about when they want to learn. The old adage about "when the student is ready, the teacher will appear" has taken on a whole new level of meaning with the aid of technology.

The blended learning approach respects learner differences in style, yet also provides the much-needed social interaction that human beings seek and enjoy. It also offers a more cost-effective method of instruction that is of equal or higher instructional value to learners than any one learning method taken on its own. In essence, blended learning is nothing more than common sense applied to e-technology, which in retrospect is something of a rarity. It means using whatever method is most suitable.

Companies that have invested heavily in e-learning will not necessarily close their training centers either. Deloitte Consulting, for example, plans to continue with classroom instruction. However, the company has used e-learning to prepare students for a company-wide classroom-based e-business course and to reinforce their learning afterwards. This program usually lasts up to seven weeks. By ''e-enabling'' the front- and back-end of the program, Deloitte Consulting has reduced the typical classroom time by 15 days.

Portals

A new subcategory of e-learning, called ''portals,'' has emerged to aggregate the thousands of e-training products that have been rushed to market. By 2002, approximately 200 portals had opened their doors, many claiming to be *the* primary destination for online learning. Such is the speed of maturity in the sector that portals are now being categorized and divided into B2C, B2B, and B2E, and horizontal, vertical, or even diagonal portals.

The most apparent benefits a portal solution provides are accessibility, flexibility, and affordability. Cornelia Weggen[10] has put forward the following reasons for considering going through a portal.

» Portals provide access to learning from multiple sources by aggregating, hosting, and distributing content. Corporate customers can pick and choose courses from a multitude of vendors and create customized programs quickly for their employees.
» Because most portals now offer their services on an outsourced application service provider (ASP) basis, no time-consuming implementations behind firewalls are necessary, and the portal can be up and running within weeks or even days.
» The total cost of a portal is generally lower than other e-learning solutions because the customer doesn't have to pay for custom-developed

content, complex installations on the intranet, or additional labor for network administration and maintenance.

» Overall, portals can help to deliver learning effectively to a geographically dispersed workforce. This lean training solution is particularly well-suited for small and medium-sized businesses that don't have the need or resources for full-scale custom course development, learning management software, or a large implementation.

More than $1bn in venture capital has poured into portal start-ups – and six companies have gone public. However, as with almost everything else in the Internet sector, portals are not a guaranteed commercial success. The recent dramatic crash of some of the more high-profile ventures in this sector illustrates how tough it has been, whilst a spate of recent successful financings by the survivors shows what it takes to really meet the online training needs of corporations.

Corporate customers want their training providers – online or otherwise – to provide somewhat more "added value" than merely being an intermediary and a creator of directories of online training offerings. The combination of unique technology and access to large amounts of training content seems to be a theme with those online training companies that are enjoying further funding.

NOTES

1 Stacey, P. (2002) "The E-Learning Value Chain and Market Map." *E-Learning*, January 25, pp. 9–14.

2 Corporate University Xchange (2002), *Pillars of e-Learning Success*. New York.

3 Hills, H. (2002) "The Shape of the E-Learning Marketplace – its Products, Services, and Customers." *Training Journal*, February.

4 Brandon Hall (2002) "*Learning Management Systems and Learning Content Management Systems Demystified.*" http://www.brandonhall.com/public/resources/lms_lcms/

5 Adkins, S. (2002) Market Analysis of the 2002 US E-Learning Industry. Brandon Hall.

6 Boulton, P. (2002) "How Organisations are Using E-Learning: a Snapshot of the Current State of 190 Organisations in Australia." Monash University Working Papers.

7 Pecaut, D. (2001) "The Future of E-Learning." Remarks to the Learning Partnership, Toronto, June 7. http://www.tlp.on.ca/Remarks/Thefutureofelearning.html

8 Curran, L. (2001) "Going Mobile." *e-learn Magazine*, September 11. http://www.elearnmag.org/subpage/sub_page.cfm?article_pk=1880&page_number_nb=1&title=FEATURE%20STORY

9 Hofmann, J. (2001) "Peer-to-Peer – the Next Hot Trend in E-Learning?" *Learning Circuits*. http://www.learningcircuits.org/2002/jan2002/hofmann.html

10 Weggen, C. (2001) "Learning Portals – Who Needs Them? "*Learning Circuits*. http://www.learningcircuits.org/sep2000/weggen.html

In Practice – E-Training and Development Success Stories

This chapter includes case studies of:

» IBM;
» ScottishPower;
» Yamatake Building Systems (YBS); and
» Cisco Systems.

IBM

IBM was incorporated in the State of New York on June 15, 1911 as the Computing-Tabulating-Recording Company. But its origins can be traced back to 1890, during the height of the industrial revolution, when the US was experiencing waves of immigration. The US Census Bureau knew its traditional methods of counting would no longer be adequate for measuring the population, so it sponsored a contest to find a more efficient means of tabulating census data.

The winner was Herman Hollerith, a German immigrant and Census Bureau statistician, whose punchcard tabulating machine used an electric current to sense holes in punchcards and keep a running total of data. Capitalizing on his success, Hollerith formed the Tabulating Machine Co. in 1896.

For 60 years the company grew, alongside the emerging IT industry, until it became one of the world's largest and most profitable businesses, enjoying a dominant share of virtually the whole of the computer market of the day.

IBM came into the PC era, having settled one anti-trust action and fighting another. It had acquired a reputation for arrogance. It believed it was the best, but the trouble with that belief was that change is difficult to implement from within with an "it ain't broke so why fix it" mentality. The company badly fumbled desktop computing, handing over the two most critical PC architectural control points – the systems software and the microprocessor – to Microsoft and Intel. Despite, or perhaps because of, its efforts in research – which produced five Nobel Prize winners in physics – the company plunged into a disastrous series of losses and its very survival was frequently called into question.

Louis V. Gerstner, Jr arrived as IBM's chairman and CEO on April 1, 1993. For the first time in the company's history IBM had found a leader from outside its ranks. Gerstner had been chairman and CEO of RJR Nabisco for four years and had previously spent 11 years as a top executive at American Express. Gerstner also brought with him a customer-oriented sensibility and the strategic-thinking expertise that he had honed through years as a management consultant at McKinsey & Co.

Management training became a critical business issue at IBM, and became part of its strategy for adapting to its fight back to prosperity. Unsurprisingly for a company at the heart of the new economy, e-learning is a crucial component of the company's overall training approach.

In 1997, Gerstner commissioned research to find out which qualities separated the best executives from the rest. A year later he initiated a similar study for managers. In both cases, the ability to coach employees effectively turned up right at the top of the list as an essential skill for good management.

IBM bought into a coaching methodology created by former racing driver Sir John Whitmore. Whitmore's model, "GROW," consists of four stages: setting *G*oals; doing a *R*eality check; identifying *O*ptions and alternative strategies; and determining *W*hat needs to be done, *W*hen, and by *W*hom. For a while, IBM delivered this information to managers through training workshops, but eventually the organization came to believe that this wouldn't be enough. Coaching isn't something you can learn entirely from a book; no matter how good the book is – you need practical experience.

IBM felt that completing simulations based on the GROW model would be valuable pre-work to get trainees up to speed on coaching before their classroom training. They wrote up the scenarios for the simulation and then set the process up on their intranet. Students come online, read the scenario, and are invited to react to the situation in one of a number of ways. Based on their answers, students click "see analysis" to read a summary of the consequences of all the actions they have taken so far in the scenario or "consult expert" to read a story from an IBM coaching expert. Alternatively, instead of deciding on a course of action the user can access "pros and cons," which highlights the potential up-sides and down-sides to each approach.

This was IBM's first e-learning project and also its first major attempt at international training. In writing scripts for an international audience, the content team had to avoid any confusing Americanisms and colloquial language but still make the interactions original and interesting. Another concern was that bandwidth in remote international locations is sometimes limited. There were people halfway across the world who would be accessing the system from computer systems that were a long way from state of the art. So both video and audio were out of the question.

IBM saw its first incursion into e-learning as a success and it became the first of many. Nancy Lewis, the company's director of world management development at IBM's corporate headquarters in Armonk, New York, claims that e-learning was able to provide five times as much content at one-third of the cost. For IBM managers, e-learning is essential to the management training program. All first-line managers take part in a four-tiered strategy for training and the first six months of the program are almost exclusively online.

IBM's four-tiered e-learning program begins with groups of 24 managers entering the first tier of the program at the same time, without meeting face-to-face. Content is offered online at any time and delivered *via* the company's intranet. The tools in this tier are just-in-time performance support, with access to a substantial knowledge database of questions, answers, and sample scenarios to address common concerns such as evaluation, retention, and conflict resolution.

The second tier presents interactive learning models with more than a dozen situation simulations. Here, more seasoned IBM managers coach the new managers online. Simulations give the learners an opportunity to experience interactively topics such as business conduct, compensation and benefits, and employee skill-building. Within a handful of simulations, there are more than 5000 screens of action. Further simulations dip into areas like multicultural issues and retaining talent. Harvard Business School Publishing provided some of the content for this area and Cognitive Arts of Chicago helped create the scenarios.

Collaboration begins as the managers enter the third tier. Using Lotus Learning Space, the groups of managers that have been moving up through the tiers interact and solve problems as a team.

The fourth tier assembles colleagues from a particular management class for a week of in-class lab activities. The difference is that there are no lectures. Anything that previously would have been delivered as a lecture or pure content will have been delivered online, and learners will have passed an online test on that content. Learners also have to complete work prior to attending the lab. The lab time is spent in activities that require the managers to solve problems as a team, face-to-face. This fourth tier typically follows six months of e-learning experiences.

Before the e-learning program, managers had to travel to attend in-class training courses during the first six months of management development. Now all of it occurs online, when and where the student desires to learn.

IBM has become so enamored with the whole process that it has entered the e-learning market itself with two types of offerings. IBM Mindspan Solutions, launched in 2000, just three years after IBM had tested the water itself, aims to help transform any business by making effective e-learning an integral part of the organization. It offers a complete e-learning service that combines consulting, world-class custom-content development, and e-learning delivery and support. In addition, IBM offers hundreds of courses that are available in Web-delivered and virtual-classroom formats, together with hands-on laboratories and live instructors.

IBM wanted a worldwide system to address the continuous skill development of all its employees in 160 countries, and it has achieved this by setting up a global virtual university. Its "campus" claims to embrace the world's largest intranet e-learning application, with 19,000 classroom, conference, and distributed-learning courses and 185,000 registered students. Its e-training programs have won national and international awards and, according to IBM, have already saved it $200mn. (To read more on IBM's e-learning programs, see Professor Schank's book.[1])

Time-line

» **1890** – Herman Hollerith starts his business.
» **1896** – Hollerith wins US Census Bureau competition and sets up Tabulating Machine Co.
» **1911** – Charles R. Flint, a noted trust organizer, engineered the merger of Hollerith's company with two others, Computing Scale Co. of America and International Time Recording Co. The combination was known as The Computing-Tabulating-Recording Co., or C-T-R.
» **1914** – Thomas J. Watson, the former number-two executive at National Cash Register, joined the company as general manager. He preached a positive outlook, and his favorite slogan, "Think!" became a mantra for C-T-R employees.
» **1915** – the company focused on providing large-scale, custom-built tabulating solutions for businesses, leaving the market for small office

products to others. Its name was changed to International Business Machines Corp., or IBM.

» **1939–63** – the era of innovation. IBM 701, using vacuum tubes, was introduced and by 1959 the transistor replaced valves. Thomas Watson passed on the title of president to his son, Thomas Watson, Jr, in 1956, just six months before his death.

» **1964–80** – IBM introduced the System 360, the first large "family" of computers to use interchangeable software and peripheral equipment. Rather than purchase a new system when the need and budget grew, customers could now simply upgrade parts of their hardware. It was a bold departure from the monolithic, one-size-fits-all mainframe. *Fortune* magazine dubbed it "IBM's five-billion gamble."

» **1981–92** – IBM stumbles into losses and its very survival is threatened. A number of new strategies and reorganizations are tried without success.

» **1993** – Louis V. Gerstner, Jr arrived as IBM's chairman and CEO on April 1. For the first time in the company's history, IBM had found a leader from outside its ranks. Gerstner had been chairman and CEO of RJR Nabisco for four years and had previously spent 11 years as a top executive at American Express.

» **1995** – profits restored. Profits pass the $5bn mark and return on stockholders' equity is nearly 25% and rising.

» **1997** – IBM introduces the first experiment in e-training processes to train managers, using a coaching methodology created by former racing driver Sir John Whitmore known as GROW.

» **2000** – launch of Mindspan, an e-learning platform offering a series of e-learning programs to the general management development market.

» **2001** – launch of the IBM "virtual university."

» **2002** – IBM has 185,000 students on its e-training programs and has saved $200mn in training fees.

KEY LEARNING POINTS

» In hindsight, the first program was probably too advanced for the Web at that time. On Netscape, for instance, the system crashed constantly during testing and to get around the problem, IBM had to reprogram the entire thing and redesign the interface. The lesson here is that if a system works well on one browser, it doesn't mean it will work well on another. Test, test, and test again.

» With e-learning on the Web, the systems you build must be adaptable to the lowest-tech specifications a user might require. It's vital to know what these specs will be before building the system.

» Using proven learning models, such as Whitmore's GROW, makes the training easier to adapt for e-training programs as it has a sound pedagogical basis.

» Don't try to do everything online from the outset. Recognize the cultural learning problems that are bound to occur and plan to overcome them.

SCOTTISHPOWER

ScottishPower serves approximately seven million homes and businesses across the UK and the north-west of the US. The group's activities cover electricity generation, transmission, distribution, and supply in its UK and US operations, as well as gas supply, water, and waste-water services in the UK and mining in the US. ScottishPower and its subsidiaries comprise one of the 12 largest electricity groups in the world, with a market capitalization of £9bn (approximately $12.6bn) and over 22,000 employees.

ScottishPower's policy relating to investing in learning evolved in response to changes in its operating environment. Until 1990, Scottish-Power was a publicly owned, State-driven utility with a geographically specific market, but in 1990 the electricity industry was deregulated and ScottishPower was privatized. In other words, after 1990 Scottish-Power had to operate as an investor-owned electricity company in a highly competitive, and increasingly global, marketplace.

The changes associated with privatization generated many challenges for ScottishPower and its employees. Downsizing inevitably placed pressures on employees. Fewer people were expected to do more work, creating additional demands on employees, and capping salaries did little to encourage incentive. More than at any other point in its history, ScottishPower needed to be the type of organization that could change quickly to capture emerging opportunities.

The company required employees who were not only able to change with the organization and its customers, but who were also *willing* to do so. In order to create favorable conditions for building an improvement-oriented workforce that was open to change, both during and after privatization, ScottishPower began to place greater emphasis on staff training and development so as to affirm employees' skills.

ScottishPower set out to foster within the company a culture of lifelong learning that:

» increased motivation and flexibility across the workforce;
» benefited both ScottishPower staff and members of the community;
» improved economic development in socially deprived areas; and
» enhanced the leadership skills of future ScottishPower managers.

ScottishPower's entire approach to training and development was, and continues to be, built on three of its core values: providing a positive working environment; creating a culture based on teamwork and leadership; and supporting the communities in which the company operates. As much as possible, ScottishPower accomplished these objectives simultaneously.

ScottishPower recognized early that the key to sustaining itself lay in retaining quality staff who were given ongoing opportunities to refresh and enhance their skills and knowledge. To facilitate life-long learning, ScottishPower established a network of open learning centers and created ScottishPower Learning (SPL), a separate division of ScotttishPower which operates in three sites in the UK. This was a joint initiative between ScottishPower and the company's trade unions that was intended to enable people in the community to learn at the company's training and learning centers. Whilst the centers were initially created for the exclusive use of ScottishPower staff, to study languages, develop computer skills, and gain vocational and other qualifications, the centers are now open to members of employees' families and to others in the community, including schools, small businesses, local charities, youth groups, and unemployed adults.

Today, ScottishPower has 51 open learning centers spread across the UK, with eight more being developed in the US. Over 75% of ScottishPower staff, their families, and people of all ages from the local communities, have made use of an open learning center.

ScottishPower claims the following benefits and effects for its open learning programs.

» **Individual learners in the community:**
  » enhance their employability, life-skills, attitudes, and behaviors;
  » gain skill-based qualifications;
  » build confidence to pursue their ambitions;
  » develop skills in demand amongst employers;
  » have supervised work experience;
  » expand their career options;
  » participate in training and development programs that match their individual needs;
  » see how they come across to employers; and
  » gain nationally recognized vocational and City & Guilds qualifications through their work.
» **Employees:**
  » enhance their employability, life-skills, attitudes, and behaviors by getting involved in the learning experience of others;
  » gain recognition;
  » take charge of their own training and development;
  » follow their own agenda and create their own opportunities;
  » participate in training and development programs that match their individual needs;
  » learn out of desire; and
  » unleash their potential.
» **ScottishPower:**
  » taps into its employees' creativity;
  » captures employees' imagination and ideas;
  » positions itself for competitiveness and growth;
  » builds positive community relations;
  » contributes to economic development in socially deprived areas;

> » builds the leadership skills of future ScottishPower managers; and
> » enhances motivation and flexibility across the workforce.

ScottishPower has measurement and evaluation processes in place for all of its online learning activities. Program evaluations differ according to the nature and intended results of each program. At a strategic level, ScottishPower is careful to ensure that its SPL activities combine to meet the company's overall business objectives, and that any new areas of involvement fit closely with its strategic objectives.

Time-line

» **1990** – ScottishPower created when UK energy market was privatized.
» **1996** – ScottishPower created ScottishPower Learning (SPL), a separate division of ScotttishPower intended to enable people in the community to learn at the company's training and learning centers.
» **1998** – turnover hits £3.13bn (approximately $4.4trn).
» **2001** – ScottishPower wins Global Best Award for Corporate Leadership in recognition of the success of its online learning's "School-to-Work Education and Training Programs."[2]
» **2002** – group turnover grows to £6.3bn (approximately $8.8trn). Operating profit hits £944mn (approximately $1.3bn) and company wins award for best company for customer satisfaction in the UK domestic gas market.

KEY LEARNING POINTS

» Link e-training and development programs closely to the recognized and agreed strategy of the whole business.
» Make the process as inclusive as possible to ensure maximum opportunity for learning experiences to be reinforced and shared.
» Seek external recognition for e-learning programs, as this can lend extra internal credibility.
» Evaluate the effectiveness of e-learning initiatives and publicize findings widely.

YAMATAKE BUILDING SYSTEMS (YBS)

In Japan, the year 2000 is referred to as the "first year of the e-learning era."[3] Since then, the number of major corporations, venture firms, and US-owned companies entering the e-learning market has rapidly increased. Studies conducted by various US organizations, including IDC and Merrill Lynch, predict that the market will expand annually by 20% or more.

E-learning holds benefits for top management and HR education, not only because it can be used to cut training costs, but also because it is an efficient and effective tool for training employees. In Japan, however, the degree of understanding and experience differs greatly according to company size and industry type. Major corporations, particularly those in the information-systems sector, provide most e-learning implementation case studies. In recent months, companies in other fields, such as the financial and medical sectors, have also begun to implement e-learning programs – most of these, however, are also major corporations.

YBS's primary business is building automation systems. It handles development, production, sales, installation, engineering, maintenance, and management. The company has also made use of its building automation technology to create businesses dealing with energy conservation, to assist other companies in obtaining ISO 14000 certification, and to build care-giving businesses.

There was an urgent problem that first led the company to consider adopting e-learning technology. Its training center located in Shonan was only able to train a maximum of 2000 employees annually, but the needs of its technicians, partner firms, and authorized dealers required that nearly 5000 employees be trained each year. YBS saw e-learning as the only way to solve the capacity problem and in 1999 it created a cross-company "YeS promotion team" for the purpose of implementing an e-learning system for itself, its partners, and its dealers. Efforts to establish this team were led by the company's top executives and managers, and after examining various options, they decided to go first with Lotus Learning Space intranet software.

YBS installed the system on a trial basis in the autumn of 2000 and used it to train freshmen staff who had been with the company for six months. While many other companies also instal e-learning systems on a trial basis, YBS went one step further by conducting a statistical analysis of the results instead of merely preparing a questionnaire for participants. Based on this experience, the company defined e-learning patterns for the areas in which the system was to be applied, taking into account the special features of the training program and the cost and time required.

In short, practical training is offered at YBS's training center as usual. Courses that rely primarily on classroom-type studies include Web-based training (WBT) content (kept to the minimum necessary), combined with existing textbooks. Content best delivered *via* the Web is, however, outsourced to external content developers.

YBS not only develops its own content and manages its own e-learning system, it also keeps a record of progress in order to boost employee awareness and skills, and it subscribes to various learning services for its staff, such as English language and book-keeping. Although technically-oriented staff dominate the industry that it's in, YBS also provides e-learning opportunities to managers and non-technical staff in an attempt to create an enlightened corporate environment. Deadlines are set for the use of e-training programs, and if employees do not take advantage of these services they lose opportunities to do so in the future. YBS's intranet-based e-learning portal site offers two areas: "YeS I" features content developed in-house; and "YeS II" offers content bought in from outside suppliers. These efforts were designed to make it possible for the company to instal a fully-fledged e-learning system that would make it possible to deliver e-learning courses to the entire workforce.

There are two principal factors that have enabled YBS to achieve successful results: a strong commitment by top management; and a keen interest of related staff in information gathering and their quick response. The top management did not just simply implement e-learning in a strategic manner; whenever managers visited a regional office they promoted the technology in order to instill broad interest.

Furthermore, the department in charge of e-learning gathered a large volume of information on the subject, conducted its own inspections, attempted to develop the technology in-house, and made other efforts to learn more about e-learning content in order to create it. YBS plans to continue to broaden and improve its WBT course menu in the future.

Time-line

» **1998** – YBS recognizes it has a capacity problem when it comes to training. Its physical training facilities can handle 2000 people a year but it needs to get 5000 people through.

» **1999** – cross-company "YeS promotion team" created for the purpose of implementing an e-learning system.

» **2000** – Lotus Learning Space intranet software installed on a trial basis and used to train freshmen staff who had been with the company for six months.

» **2001** – fully-fledged e-learning system installed, which would make it possible to deliver e-learning courses to the entire workforce.

» **2002** – YBS starts to evaluate the impact of its e-learning program.

KEY LEARNING POINTS

» Having a clear business reason for introducing a change to e-training systems makes the process more acceptable to employees.

» Commitment from the top of the organization is vital.

» Offering both company-required training and personal development programs speeds up the technology utilization.

» Using a proven platform, such as Lotus Learning Space, reduces the potential for initial problems and gets users into programs faster.

CISCO SYSTEMS

Cisco Systems has bought more than 70 companies over the past 15 years and set aside a further $10bn for future deals. William Nuti, senior vice-president, in an interview for *Sunday Business* in April 2000, is quoted as saying, "management consultants who do this for a living come to Cisco to learn how to acquire and integrate companies successfully." It has to be said that most important research studies of the past 30 years into mergers and acquisitions, as a strategy to create shareholder value, have detected little evidence to be quite as sanguine as Nuti.

Some six months before Nuti's newspaper interview, Cisco's internal training scheme was reaching crisis point. This was not because of a problem with the quality of the training, but with the sheer quantity. The company was growing exponentially and could not train its expanding workforce fast enough.

Until 1999, Cisco used standard, instructor-led training, sending employees to the classroom. Since then, it has adopted e-learning, using the company intranet to deliver training direct to the desktop. By January 2001,[4] Cisco had reached the inflection point, where more than half its training programs were delivered over the net.

Cisco has also scaled up its training, offering its internal courses over the Internet to its external marketing partners. Scaling-up the volume of training in this way, Cisco has discovered that it can save literally millions of dollars. Not only does the company save the cost of airfares and hotel bills, but also staff are more productive because they spend less time away from their desks. Before e-learning, sales staff spent six days a year away on product training, and technical staff 12 days a year.

Teaching 100 people on one topic, Cisco has to pay the instructor four times and pay travel costs 100 times. If the company teaches the same 100 people via the Internet, it only pays the instructor once and there are no travel costs. Unlike traditional training, costs don't rise proportionately with the number of people trained.

There was concern among employees that the introduction of e-learning would force employees to catch up on coursework outside working hours. In the event, more than 80% of training is still done during the working day. There is no regulation of when staff do their training. People do it at times to suit themselves, dialling in to do an hour and breaking it into manageable chunks, like taking three meals a day.

The training programs are delivered in two ways, either as Cisco TV, broadcast to the desk, or as video-on-demand. Staff will be informed that at nine o'clock on Monday morning there is a company broadcast on the latest high-speed gigabit router. They can click in and watch it like an Open University TV program. The program is videotaped and stored for staff to dial into and replay at any time. The broadcast is interactive, allowing staff to ask questions, either directly or *via* a moderator who summarizes all questions to prevent the flow being interrupted.

Cisco plans to have 100% of its courses online. To implement the enterprise-wide e-learning strategy, Cisco put together a program that stores each part of a lesson in a reusable format on a database, from which small chunks of information can be pulled out on demand to serve training needs. The program uses XML metadata tagging, based on the emerging IMS Global Learning Consortium standard, to ensure it is user-compatible with the other programs and systems in the industry. This system allows for the creation of a single repository of information that can be used in training, documentation, and other capacities.

Cisco spends $40mn a year on training in Europe, and claims that the cost savings of e-learning can be quantified in tens of millions. But the improved quality of training and the productivity gains have broader implications. The move towards e-learning has been instrumental in helping Cisco to hit its very aggressive revenue targets. Cisco sells mainly through distributors – and e-learning means it can ensure all its partners have access to the same training at the same time. Sales staff can be tested online, to ensure they have mastered the details of Cisco's products.

The company also makes its training courses available free of charge to secondary schools and technical colleges through its Networking Academy initiative. In the UK, 500 schools and colleges use the 280 hours' worth of training material.

Cisco has its own internal department for developing learning materials, the Internet Learning Solutions Group. Everyone is involved in the course development process and meaningful user feedback is obtained before extending the application to a wider audience. Cisco always includes a group of non-technical employees to review applications, believing that they would give an unbiased opinion of the software.

But the company is not averse to outsourcing if others have better solutions. For example, it wanted to be able to use its content across a wide range of training programs without involving mammoth amounts of rewriting. Cisco found and used Evolution, a new development and delivery tool produced by start-up company OutStart that enables developers to author e-learning content in an application that automates the creation, tagging, storing, and searching of objects in a database environment. Instead of a traditional flat file in a desktop application, such as Microsoft Word, Evolution is a Web-form, database-driven tool. Whilst it was risky being an early-adopter, the payback was colossal.

From a financial standpoint, because of the capability to reuse content and a reduction in content development time, Cisco expects to see a 500% return on investment. For example, it recently developed a course in half the time and the budget by reusing learning objects, and over the past year it has developed more than 130 courses, 2500 lessons, and 20,000 reusable learning objects. Likewise, with 150 authors spread throughout Cisco and its external development partners, the concept of a database-driven authoring environment has caught on quickly.

Time-line

» **1968** - December 9, Doug Engelbart and a small team of researchers from the Stanford Research Institute stunned the computing world with an extraordinary demonstration at a San Francisco computer conference. They debuted: the computer mouse; graphical user interface (GUI); display editing; integrated text and graphics; hyper-documents; and two-way videoconferencing with shared work-spaces. These concepts and technologies were to become the cornerstones of modern interactive computing.

» **1981** - Bill Yeager produced a stable router. Yeager's work involved the development of a unique, stand-alone operating system and service programs for a router that could efficiently handle routing of packets for diverse protocols among a number of networks connected to the router.

» **1984** - Sandy Lerner (Economics MS, 1981) and Leonard Bosack (CS MS, 1981) founded Cisco Systems. Lerner was director of computer facilities for Stanford's Graduate School of Business and Bosack was director of computer facilities for Stanford's Department of Computer Science.

» **1986** - Lerner and Bosack license the software developed by Yeager and others on behalf of Cisco Systems through the Stanford Office of Technology Licensing.

» **1987** - Cisco receives first and only venture capital funding, from Sequoia, and establishes corporate headquarters in Menlo Park, California, which houses its 10 employees.

» **1989** - first OEM agreement signed with NET, and 174th employee signed on.
» **1990** - Cisco makes initial public offering on Feb 16. Sales of $69mn; 254 employees.
» **1992** - Cisco opens in Japan and publishes its first advertisement.
» **1993** - first acquisition, Crescendo Communications, for $89mn.
» **1995** - John Chambers becomes CEO. Sales of $2.23bn; 3479 employees.
» **1997** - Cisco first appears in *Fortune 500*. Ten-thousandth employee hired on February 4.
» **1999** - thirty-eighth consecutive quarter of revenue and profits growth. Cisco acquires 18 companies and minority stakes in 38 others. The company reaches the limit of conventional training methods.
» **2000** - e-learning programs launched.
» **2001** - Cisco has more e-learning programs than conventional, live tutor-led programs.
» **2002** - Cisco controls almost two-thirds of the global market for routers and switches that link networks and power the Internet. It also makes network access servers and management software. Not content to dominate the computer networking market, Cisco competes with giants such as Nortel and Lucent in the telecommunications sector, with products designed to accommodate data, voice, and video traffic.
» **2002** - Cisco Systems Canada wins 2002 National Award for Learning Technologies in the Workplace.

KEY LEARNING POINTS

» Keep e-training content consistent. Initially, course developers thought that training content had to be different for classroom-based and e-learning delivery. Clearly, e-learning needs such features as animation and audio to keep learners engaged, but course content and structure are basically the same for online and classroom-based courses - if the instructional design is good.

» Involve stakeholders. That includes developers, editorial staff, proofreaders, and graphic designers, as well as user groups. Many companies fail to include all team members in the process, which hinders the company's ability to create a streamlined system that's acceptable to all.

» Don't be afraid to use innovative suppliers, if they are really committed to their new tools.

» Don't force students to learn at your pace. Give them outcome targets and let *them* set the pace.

NOTES

1 Schank, R. (2002) *Designing World Class E-Learning – How IBM, GE, Harvard Business School, and Columbia University are Succeeding at E-Learning*. McGraw-Hill.

2 Conference Board of Canada (2001) "Effective Practices in Building Skills to Enhance Corporate and Community Capacity." Case study 43. www.conferenceboard.ca/education/pdf/ScottishPower.pdf

3 Oshima, A. (2001) "How E-Learning is Being Used in Japan." SRIC Report 2001, vol. 7, no. 1. ww.learning-technology.net/en/reference/member/article.htm

4 Cisco Systems E-Learning Case Studies, (2002). http://www.cisco.com/warp/public/10/wwtraining/elearning/educate/cases.htm

Key Concepts and Thinkers

The concepts and thinkers that underpin e-training and development are both old and new. Some, indeed, are very new as the foundations are less than a decade old, and the language used is almost entirely new. This chapter contains:

» a glossary of the most common terms; and
» key writers and thinkers and their related concepts.

GLOSSARY

Advanced distributed learning (ADL) – initiative of the US Department of Defense to achieve interoperability across computer and Internet-based learning courseware through the development of a common technical framework, which contains content in the form of reusable learning objects.

Asynchronous learning – learning in which interaction between teachers and students occurs with a time delay, so that students can work at their own pace.

Asynchronous transfer mode (ATM) – a network technology for high-speed transfer of data in packets of a fixed size, allowing for smooth transmission to support real-time video and voice applications.

Authoring tool – a software application or program that allows people to create their own online e-learning courseware.

Blended learning – training that combines aspects of online and face-to-face instruction.

Broadband – telecommunication that provides multiple channels of data over a single communications medium. The greater the bandwidth, the greater the carrying capacity. Lack of bandwidth is a key factor in limiting the wider use of the Internet in certain areas of the world.

Bulletin board system (BBS) – an online community run on a host computer which users can dial into or log onto. Users can post messages on discussion boards, send and receive e-mail, chat with other users, and upload and download files.

Chat – real-time text-based communication, an online service used in e-training for student questions, instructor feedback, and group discussion.

Collaborative tools – allow learners to work with others *via* e-mail, threaded discussions, or chats, either in real time or with a time delay.

Computer-based training (CBT) – a teaching process in which students learn a specific set of skills by executing training programs on a computer. CBT is very effective for computer applications training. Also called CAL (computer-assisted learning) and CAI (computer-assisted instruction).

Content – the intellectual property and know-how used for e-learning, including text, audio, video, animation, and simulation content.

Content management system (CMS) – system used to store large amounts of data so that it can be easily retrieved. CMS works by indexing elements of training materials within a database, using built-in search capabilities.

Courseware – any type of instructional or educational course delivered *via* a software program or over the Web.

Discussion forums – places where people can post messages on a particular topic and receive replies at a later date. The Internet equivalent of a notice board.

Distance learning – instruction provided by a live teacher, separated in place and time.

E-book – software that organizes learning material into lessons or chapters in the same way as a conventional hard-copy book, but delivery is on a computer screen.

E-learning – anytime, anywhere electronic or computer-supported learning using Web and Internet technologies to create, enable, and deliver. Also called Web-based training (WBT).

Evaluation – any systematic method for gathering information about the impact and effectiveness of a learning event, usually with a view to improving the process.

Graphical user interface (GUI) – computer interface using icons or pictures; for example, Macintosh and Windows® software.

HTML (hypertext mark-up language) – code used to create and access documents on the Web.

Instructional management systems (IMS) – a set of technical specifications defining how learning materials will be exchanged over the Internet and how organizations and individual learners will use them. Initiated by Educom and developed through a consortium of academic, commercial, and government organizations. The consortium's goal is the adoption of a set of open standards for Internet-based education.

Instructor-led training (ILT) – usually refers to traditional classroom training, in which an instructor teaches a class, real or virtual, to a room of students.

Internet-based training – training delivered primarily by network technologies such as e-mail, newsgroups, and so forth. The term is often used synonymously with Web-based training (WBT).

Knowledge management – collecting, organizing, and storing knowledge and experiences of individuals and groups within an organization and making it available to others in the organization. The information is stored in a dedicated database called a knowledge base. It can help prevent energy being wasted on reinventing the wheel.

Learning content management system (LCMS) – software that allows trainers to manage both the administrative and content-related functions of training.

Learning management system (LMS) – software that makes routine the administration of training events, managing the logging-on of registered users, course catalogues, recording data from learners, and providing management reports on training events.

Learning objects – self-contained pieces of training content that can be assembled to create many different courses and curricula, much the same way as bricks can be put together to create many different structures. Their purpose is to increase the flexibility of training and make updating courses easier to manage.

Learning portal – a Website offering consolidated access to learning and training resources from multiple sources. Also known as content aggregators, distributors, or hosts.

Learning service provider (LSP) – a specialist organization offering learning management and training delivery software on a hosted or rental basis.

M-learning (mobile learning) – learning that takes place via mobile phones, personal digital assistants (PDAs), or laptop computers.

MP3 – a format for music file compression that allows users to download music over the Internet.

MPEG (moving picture experts group) – a standard for compressing digital video images.

Open learning – an educational environment that provides learners with choices about media, place of study, pace of study, support mechanisms, and entry and exit points.

Peer-to-peer network (P2P) – a network that enables users to connect their computers and share files directly with other users without having to go through a centralized server.

Portal – a Website that acts as a "doorway" to the Internet or a portion of the Internet, usually tailored to the needs of a particular community.

Real time – telephone calls and videoconferencing are examples of real-time applications. E-mail, on the other hand, is usually not instantaneous, even when people are on the same intranet. Real-time information needs to be processed and delivered almost instantaneously, arriving in the order in which it was sent.

Return on investment (ROI) – a ratio of the benefit or profit received from a given investment to the cost of the original investment. In e-learning, if the benefit is $100 and the cost is $1000, then the ROI is 10% (100 + 1000%100). ROI is most often calculated by comparing the measurable results of training – for example, an increase in output such as units produced or sales calls made, or a decrease in error rate – to the cost of providing the training.

Reusable information object (RIO) – a collection of content, practice, and assessment items assembled around a single learning objective.

SCORM (shareable content object reference model) – a set of standards that, when applied to training material, produces small, reusable learning objects. The idea behind SCORM came out of the US Defense Department's ADL initiative.

Self-paced learning – training in which the learner determines the pace and timing of content delivery.

Streaming media – audio or video files played as they are being downloaded over the Internet, rather than users having to wait for the entire file to be downloaded first.

Subject matter expert – someone who is recognized as having proficiency in a particular subject or field.

Synchronous – communication in which interaction between learner and instructor takes place simultaneously. Also called real-time.

Telecourse – training delivered *via* television, which generally includes a textbook, study guide, faculty manual, and other instructional materials, such as those delivered by the Open University.

Template – a set of tools or forms that allows training content to be developed quickly.

Threaded discussion – a series of linked online messages that are "threaded" together by topic.

Uniform resource locator (URL) – the address of a document or Web-page on the Internet.

Value-added services – a term used to describe the whole gamut of services offered by companies in the e-learning industry. Amongst others, they include program design and development, delivery, progress monitoring, evaluation, and Internet hosting.

Virtual university – a higher education institution that has no physical classrooms. Instruction at a virtual university is delivered to students from a distance, by television, distance-learning materials, and Internet resources.

Web-based training (WBT) – delivering training materials *via* a Web-browser over the Internet or an intranet. A term used more or less interchangeably with e-learning.

Whiteboarding – placing shared documents and other materials onto part of a computer screen, leaving the rest of the screen free for other applications. For example, putting a picture, chart, or table on-screen during a videoconference. The user works with familiar tools to mark up the electronic whiteboard, much like with a traditional wall-mounted board.

XML (extensible mark-up language) – Web-page coding language that enables Website designers to program their own mark-up commands as a substitute for standard HTML commands.

KEY THINKERS

Richard Bandler & John Grinder

Richard Bandler and John Grinder were the first to introduce the concept of neuro-linguistic programming (NLP). The three elements of NLP can be described as follows:

1 **Neuro** – considers our brain patterns and the ways in which we prefer to communicate.

2 **Linguistics** – refers to our speech patterns, which are linked to the way we prefer to communicate. NLP suggests we should mirror the preferred methods of those we are trying to communicate with, as this will result in more effective communication.

3 **Programming** – suggests that people can be programmed to respond to certain events. Frequent and positive feedback, for example, will help embed a particular type of behavior.

The ideas behind NLP are the foundation of many of the benefits claimed for e-learning over conventional classroom-based learning. Learning requires attention. In order to be effective, training has to get a person's attention and hold it. Unfortunately, the neural systems in the brain that control attention and store information in the memory get tired very quickly (within minutes). They need to rest every three to five minutes, or they will become less responsive. They recover quickly, but training has to work with this quick fatigue/boredom pattern for the person to learn efficiently.

Training that is patterned to move from one set to another provides the most effective learning model. The patterns those neural sets respond best to involve intermingling different types of information and using different areas of the brain. Neural systems are interrelated and work together to form memory, which is the basis of new learning. The goal of a training method is to form memory in each neural system. So information that is designed and presented in a way that moves from neural system to neural system creates more effective learning.

In addition to catering for these basic needs of neural systems, training should incorporate other elements, such as interaction, imagery, and feedback. The keys to successful ''management'' of NLP, to which e-learning is ideally suited, include:

» **varying the types of content** – images, sounds, and text work together to build memory in several areas of the brain and result in better retention of the material;

» **creating interaction that engages the attention** – games and activities that involve the manipulation of data on-screen create more interest, which in turn builds better retention.

» **providing immediate feedback** – e-learning courses can build in immediate feedback to correct misunderstood material and the more immediate the feedback, the better, as each step of learning builds on the previous step.
» **encouraging interaction with other e-learners and an e-instructor** – chat rooms, discussion boards, e-mail, and building an online community all offer effective interaction for e-learners, which significantly influences the success of online programs by catering for neural systems.

Books by Bandler and Grinder include:
» *The Structure of Magic – a Book About Communication and Change* (1980). Science & Behavior Books, Palo Alto, California.
» *The Structure of Magic II – a Book About Language and Therapy* (1990). Science & Behavior Books, Palo Alto, California.
» *Reframing – Neuro-Linguistic Programming and the Transformation of Meaning* (1989) (eds S. & C. Andreas). Real People Press, Moab, Utah.

Donald L. Kirkpatrick

Professor of the Management Institute of the University of Wisconsin, past president of the American Society for Training and Development, consultant, and prolific author. Kirkpatrick established a method for evaluating the effectiveness of training and development activities. He started developing his ideas in 1959 but these were not published in full until 1967, when his method was described in his book, *Evaluating Training Programs – The Four Levels* (second edition, 1998). The four levels are as follows.

1 Reaction – how do people feel during and immediately after the training?
2 Learning – how much have they learned in terms of knowledge, skills, and attitudes?
3 Performance – what are they now doing differently as a result of the learning experience?
4 Organizational results – what additional benefits has the organization gained?

Hamblin added a fifth level (see Hamblin, A.C. (1974) *Evaluation and Control of Training*, McGraw-Hill, Maidenhead.), which in effect was an amplification of Kirkpatrick's fourth level – ultimate value: has the training helped the organization meet its strategic mission and goals?

Kirkpatrick's levels and thinking have been imported almost intact into the evaluation models used in e-training programs. Table 8.1 below shows Kirkpatrick's ideas on how to apply the four levels (and Hamblin's fifth level) to evaluating training.

Table 8.1   Evaluating training programs.

Evaluation Level	Key factors to be measured
Reaction – how do people feel during and immediately after the training?	Was the event: enjoyable; interesting; stimulating; eye-opening?
Learning – how much have they learned in terms of knowledge, skills, and attitudes?	Have they been introduced to new concepts? Has their knowledge increased? Have their attitudes changed?
Performance – what are they now doing differently as a result of the learning experience?	Have they transferred the learning to the workplace in the form of changed attitudes and behaviors? Can they cascade the learning to others in the team?
Organizational results – what additional benefits has the organization gained?	Can the new behaviors be translated into better results for the organization? Was the training focused in the right areas? Are there other areas of the organization that could also benefit from this type of training?
Ultimate value – has the training helped the organization meet its strategic mission and goals?	Has the organization come closer to achieving its mission since the training was initiated? Are strategic goals being met or exceeded? Can the role of training be associated with total corporate performance?

Allison Rossett

Dr Allison Rossett is professor of educational technology at San Diego State University and a consultant in training and technology-based performance systems. She is the co-author of *Beyond the Podium – Delivering Training and Performance to a Digital World*, winner of the International Society for Performance Improvement (ISPI) Instructional Communications Award in 2002.

Rossett is a regular keynote speaker at conferences and events all over the world, and she teaches classes and consults on need-assessment and new-media learning and performance. Her book and free Web-tool, *First Things Fast: A Handbook for Performance Analysis*, won the International Society for Performance Improvement's Instructional Communications Award in 1999.

Other widely regarded works are her articles "Designing Under the Influence – Instructional Design for Multimedia Training" and "Training and Organizational Development – Siblings Separated at Birth," both published in *TRAINING Magazine*, and "That was a Great Class, But . . . " in *Training and Development*. Rossett teaches regularly at SDSU, including the seminar in curriculum and technology for the joint doctoral programs, the advanced seminar in instructional design, the seminar in performance technology, and the introductory educational technology class.

Rossett's e-training and development clients include Microsoft, PricewaterhouseCoopers, Hewlett-Packard, Motorola, Coca-Cola, Diamond Technology Partners, Tricon (Taco Bell, Kentucky Fried Chicken, and PizzaHut), GE Capitol, Media One, and the Getty Conservation Institute. She has served on advisory boards for IBM, Eli Lilly, and ETEC. Two projects Rossett has been closely involved with are the Bilingual Instructional Technologies Program, a successful collaboration with the San Diego County Department of Education to develop bilingual teachers in instructional design and technologies, and long-term systemic professional development programs for corporate educators at Digital Equipment Corporation and AT&T.

Roger C. Schank

Schank is one of the world's leading researchers in AI (artificial intelligence), learning theory, cognitive science, and the building of virtual learning environments. He is Distinguished Career Professor at the School of Computer Science of Carnegie Mellon University and the chief educational officer of Carnegie Mellon West. In 2000, Schank won the ASTD Distinguished Contribution to Workplace Learning and Performance Award.

Schank founded the Institute for the Learning Sciences (ILS) at Northwestern University in 1989, with support from Andersen Consulting. ILS had a staff of 170, including research and teaching faculty, programmers, content specialists, over 50 graduate students, and nearly 30 interns and visiting staff. Schank is a strong critic of today's educational system. His approach to learning, and training in a corporate setting, involves helping people learn by doing – allowing people to make mistakes in a safe learning environment and sharing war stories with leading teachers and experts. This effort has led to his highly successful role as a teacher, consultant, and lecturer, as well as developer of extremely powerful and effective multimedia training tools.

Schank is the John Evans Professor Emeritus in computer science, education, and psychology at Northwestern University. Previously he was a professor of computer science and psychology at Yale University and director of the Yale Artificial Intelligence Project. He was a visiting professor at the University of Paris VII, a faculty member at Stanford University, and research fellow at the Institute for Semantics and Cognition in Switzerland. Schank is a fellow of the AAAI and was the founder of the Cognitive Science Society and co-founder of the *Journal of Cognitive Science*. He holds a PhD in linguistics from the University of Texas.

Before founding Socratic Arts, Schank founded and served as chairman and chief technology officer of Cognitive Arts Corp., a provider of goal-based multimedia simulation training to *Fortune 500* corporations and Ivy League universities. Cognitive Arts was formed in partnership with Northwestern University to market the software initially developed at the ILS. Earlier, Schank founded and served as president of two software development companies: Cognitive Systems, Inc. (specializing in the development of knowledge-based natural language computer systems) and CompuTeach, Inc. (creating and marketing educational software for personal computers).

Schank has written over 25 books, including:

» *Designing World Class E-Learning* 2001; McGraw-Hill.
» *Engines for Education* 1995, co-written with Chip Cleary; Lawrence Erlbaum Associates.

Resources

Sets out the best resources for e-training and development, including:

- » articles;
- » books;
- » journals and magazines;
- » institutes and associations;
- » Websites;
- » research centers and think-tanks; and
- » e-learning portals.

ARTICLES

Adams, N. (1996) "Lesson from the Virtual World." *Using Technology-Delivered Learning*, p. 31.

Angus, J. (1998) "Knowledge Management – Great Concept, But What Is It?" *InformationWeek*, March 16, pp. 58–70.

Arvan, L., Ory, J., Bullock, C., Burnaska, K., & Hanson, M. (1998) "The SCALE Efficiency Projects." *Journal of Asynchronous Learning Networks*, vol. 2, issue 2, September, (1998).

Bérubé, G., Salmon, W., & Tuijnman, A. (2001) "A Report on Adult Education and Training in Canada – Learning a Living." 81-586-XIE, Ottawa, *Statistics Canada and Human Resources Development Canada*.

Bordeau, J. & Bates, A. (1996) "Instructional Design for Distance Learning." *Journal of Science Education and Technology*, no. 4, December, pp. 267–83.

Bourne, J.R. (1998) "Net-Learning Strategies for On-Campus and Off-Campus Net-Work-Enabled Learning." *Journal of Asynchronous Learning Networks*, vol. 2, no. 2.

Cheney, S. & Jarrett, L. (1998) "Up-Front Excellence for Sustainable Competitive Advantage." *Training & Development*, vol. 52, issue 6, June.

Dede, D. (1996) "The Evolution of Distance Education – Emerging Technologies and Distributed Learning." *The American Journal of Distance Education*, **10**(2), pp. 4–36.

Densford, L. (1999) "Calculating the Bottom-Line Impact of Training and Development Efforts." *Employee Benefit News*, vol. 13, issue 8, July.

Gamble, K. & Raney, B. (1998) "Teaching Through the Web." http://teachonweb.org/teaching/teaching.html.

Jonassen, D., Davidson, M., Collins, M., Campbell, J., & Hagg, B.B. (1995) "Constructivism and Computer-Mediated Communication." *The American Journal of Distance Education*, **9**(2), pp. 7–26.

Kruse, K. (1997) "Five Levels of Internet-Based Training." *Journal of Training & Development*, American Society for Training and Development, February, pp. 60–61.

Liston, C. (1997) "Using Asynchronous Learning Networks to Upgrade Skills in Manufacturing Companies." *ALN Magazine*, vol. 1, issue 1, March.

Meister, J. (1998) "Extending the Short Shelf-Life Knowledge." *Training & Development*, vol. 52, issue 6, June.

Penn State University (1997) "Guiding Principles and Practices for the Design and Development of Effective Distance Education." A Report of the Faculty Initiative funded by a grant from the AT&T Foundation.

Phillips, J.J. (1996) "ROI – The Search for Best Practices." *Journal of Training & Development*, American Society for Training and Development, February, pp. 42-7.

Salopek, J. (1998) "Coolness is a State of Mind." *Training & Development*, vol. 52, issue 11, November.

Turgeon, A. (1997) "Implication of Web-Based Technology for Engaging Students in a Learning Society." *Journal of Public Service and Outreach*, 2(2), 32-7.

BOOKS

Bartolic-Zlomislic, S. (1998) *The Costs & Benefits of Tele-Learning – Two Case Studies*. University of British Columbia, Distance Education & Technology, Canada.

Beer, V. (2000) *The Web Learning Fieldbook – Using the World Wide Web to Build Workplace Learning*. Jossey-Bass, San Francisco.

Broadbent, B. (2002) *The ABC of E-Learning: Reaping the Benefits and Avoiding the Pitfalls*. Jossey-Bass, San Francisco.

Brunner, C. & Tally, W. (1999) *The New Media Literacy Handbook – An Educator's Guide to Bringing Learning into the Classroom*. Anchor, New York.

Cairncross, F. (1997) *The Death of Distance – How the Communications Revolution Will Change our Lives*. Harvard Business School Press, Boston, Massachusetts.

Clark, R. (1999) *Developing Technical Training – A Structured Approach for Developing Classroom and Computer-Based Instructional Materials*. International Society for Predominance Improvement, Washington, DC.

Davenport, T.H. & Prusak, L. (1997) *Working Knowledge – How Organizations Manage What They Know*. Harvard Business School Press, Cambridge, Massachusetts.

Dixon, N.M. (2000) *Common Knowledge – How Companies Thrive by Sharing What They Know*. Harvard Business School Press, Boston, Massachusetts.

Driscoll, M. (1998) *Web-Based Training – Using Technology to Design Adult Learning Experiences*. Jossey-Bass, San Francisco.

Hall, B. (1997) *Web-Based Training Cookbook*. John Wiley & Sons, New York.

Horton, W.K. (2000) *Designing Web-Based Training – How to Teach Anyone, Anything, Anywhere*. John Wiley & Sons, New York.

Kruse, K. & Keil, J. (1999) *Technology-Based Training – The Art and Science of Design, Development and Delivery*. Jossey-Bass, San Francisco.

McArthur, D.J. & Lewis, M.W. (1998) *Untangling the Web – Applications of the Internet and Other Information Technologies to Higher Learning*. Rand Corporation, Santa Monica.

Rogers, E. (1995) *Diffusion of Innovations* (4th ed.). Simon & Schuster, New York.

Rosenburg, M.J. (2001) *E-Learning – Strategies for Delivering Knowledge in the Digital Age*. McGraw-Hill, New York.

Rossett, A. (2002) *The ASTD E-Learning Handbook*. McGraw-Hill, New York.

Rossett, A. (1999) *First Things Fast – A Handbook for Performance Analysis*. Jossey-Bass/Pfeiffer, San Francisco.

Ruttenbur, B.W., Spickler, G., & Lurie, S. (2000) *E-Learning – The Engine of the Knowledge Economy*. Morgan Keegan & Company, Inc., New York.

Schank, R.C. (1997) *Virtual Learning – A Revolutionary Approach to Building a Highly Skilled Workforce*. McGraw-Hill, New York.

Schreiber, D. (1998) "Organizational Technology and Its Impact on Distance Training," in *Distance Training – How Innovative Organizations Are Using Technology to Maximize Learning and Meet Business Objectives* (eds Schreiber, D.A. & Berge, Z.L.). Jossey-Bass, San Francisco.

Stevenson, N. (2001) *Distance Learning for Dummies*. IDG Books Worldwide.

Stolovitch, H. & Keeps, E. (eds) (1999) *Handbook of Human Performance Technology*. Jossey-Bass/The International Society for Performance Improvement, San Francisco.

Tiwana, A. (2000) *The Knowledge Management Toolkit – Practical Techniques for Building a Knowledge Management System*. Prentice-Hall.

JOURNALS AND MAGAZINES

American Journal of Distance Education – http://www.ed.psu/acsde/ajde/jour.asp

The Chronicle of Higher Education – http://www.chronicle.com/distance/

The Distance Education Report – http://www.distance-educator.com/

E-Learn Magazine – http://www.elearnmag.org/

Journal of Asynchronous Learning Networks – http://www.aln.org/alnweb

Journal of Computer-Assisted Learning – http://www.lancs.ac.uk/users/ktru/jcaljrnl.htm

Journal of Computer-Mediated Communication – http://www.ascusc.org/jcmc/

Journal of Continuing Higher Education – http://www.nix.oit.umass.edu~carolm/jche/

Journal of Educational Computing Research – baywood.com

Journal of Interactive Learning Research – http://www.aace.org

Journal of Interactive Multimedia in Education – http://www-jime.open.ac.uk

Journal of Instructional Science & Technology – http://www.usq.edu.au/electpub/e-jist/homepage.htm

Journal of Library Services for Distance Education – http://www.westga.edu/library/jlsde/

Journal of Technology Education – http://scholar.lib.vt.edu/ejournals/JTE/jte.html

New Horizons for Learning – http://www.newhorizons.org/

The Online Chronicle of Distance Education & Communication – http://www.fcae.nova.edu/disted/

Online Educator – http://ole.net:8081/educator

Performance Improvement Journal – http://www.ispi.org

Peterson's Guide to Distance Learning Programs - http://www.peter-sons.com/dlearn/

T + D (formerly Training and Development) - http://www.astd.org/virtual_community/td_magazine/

Technology Source - http://horizon.unc.edu/TS

THE Journal - http://www.thejournal.com

INSTITUTES AND ASSOCIATIONS

American Center for the Study of Distance Education - http://www.cde.psu.edu/ACSDE/

American Society for Training & Development (ASTD) - http://www.astd.org

Association for the Advancement of Computers in Education (AACE) - http://www.aace.org

Association for Supervision and Curriculum Development (ASCD) - http://www.ascd.org

Cisco Learning Institute - http://www.ciscolearning.org/

Computer Using Educators (CUE) - http://www.cue.org

Corporate University Xchange - http://www.corpu.com/

Distance Education Training Council (DETC) - http://www.detc.org

EduCause - http://www.educause.edu

E-Learning Vendors Association (ELVA) - http://www.elva.org/

International Centre for Distance Learning (iCDL), The Open University - http://www-icdl.open.ac.uk/

International Society for Technology in Education (ISTE) - http://www.iste.org

International Technology Education Association (ITEA) - http://www.iteawww.org

International Teleconferencing Association (ITCA) - http://www.itca.org/

MIT Center for Support for Research in Technology-Facilitated Learning - http://www-caes.mit.edu/

National Education Association (NEA) - http://www.nea.org

National Science Teachers Association (NSTA) - http://www.nsta.org/

Open University – http://www.open.ac.uk/

Society for Applied Learning and Technology (SALT) - http://www.salt.org

UK Higher Education Learning Technology Support Network (LTSN) – http://www.ltsn.ac.uk/

University of Wisconsin Distance Learning Clearinghouse – http://www.uwex.edu/disted/home.html

US Distance Learning Association (USDLA) – http://www.usdla.org

Web Base Information Center – http://www.filename.com/wbt/

The Wellspring – an online community of distance educators – http://wellspring.isinj.com

World Association for Online Education – http://www.waoe.org

WEBSITES

Cisco Systems (site has commercialized resources for e-learning, including case studies) – http://www.cisco.com/warp/public/10/wwtraining/elearning/

Cybrary (the e-learning Cybrary is an ontology-based collection of annotated links to e-learning sites, news, documents, portals, and other e-learning resources available on the Web) – http://www.co-i-l.com/elearning

eclipse (a comprehensive "one-stop resource" for e-learning that provides structured access to thousands of links of *selected* and *reviewed* e-learning) – http://www.e-learningcentre.co.uk/eclipse/Default.htm

e-learningguru ("how to" articles on e-learning) – http://www.e-learningguru.com/articles.htm

e-learning hub (articles, FAQs, book reviews) – http://www.e-learninghub.com/index.html

e-learning (directory covering whole European market) – http://www.elearning-directory.com/

eSocrates, Inc. – http://www.esocrates.com/

Learning Post – http://www.elearningpost.com/

Lguide (reviews of e-learning programs and providers) – http://www.lguide.com

MCCCD Learning Communities – http://www.mcli.dist.maricopa.edu/monograph/index.html

North Central Regional Educational Laboratory (NCREL) (NCREL manages the e-learning knowledge base, which provides a review and synthesis of current literature on e-learning) – http://www.ncrel.org/tech/elearn/framework.htm

Start4All (extensive listing of e-learning Websites) – http://e-learning.start4all.com/

UK LearningNet (the UK learning net pages, discussion groups, and more, all about learning and teaching) – http://www.uk-learning.net/

RESEARCH CENTERS AND THINK-TANKS

Brandon Hall (established in 1993 to provide independent, objective information about using technology for learning) – http://www.brandon-hall.com/

The Concord Consortium – http://www.concord.org

Institute for Computer-Based Learning, Heriot-Watt University, UK – http://www.icbl.hw.ac.uk

Institute for Learning Sciences, Northwestern University – http://www.ils.nwu.edu

Institute for Learning Technologies, Columbia University – http://www.ilt.columbia.edu

Knowledge Media Institute, Open University – http://kmi.open.ac.uk

The MASIE Center (an international e-lab and think-tank located in Saratoga Springs, NY) – http://www.masie.com/

National Center for Supercomputer Applications, University of Illinois – http://www.nsca.edu

Virtual Reality & Education Lab, East Carolina University – http://eastnet.educ.ecu.edu/vr/vrel.htm

E-LEARNING PORTALS

ActiveEducation – http://www.activeeducation.com

Adult University – http://www.adultu.com

AvidLearn.com – http://www.avidlearn.com/

Beginners.co.uk – http://www.beginners.co.uk

BlueU – http://www.blueu.com/

Business Training Partnership – http://www.btp.uk.com

Click2Learn.com – http://www.click2learn.com.

Click2Train.com Vehicle Training – http://www.click2train.com

Corpedia Training Technologies – http://www.corpedia.com

Coursebridge – http://www.coursebridge.com

CyberClasses - http://www.cyberclasses.com/
CyberU - http://www.cyberu.com/home.asp
Distance-Educator.com - http://distance-educator.com/
Earthnet Institute - http://www.ed2go.com/earthnet
easycando - http://www.easycando.com
e-learn - http://www.e-learn.uk.com
Elementk - http://www.elementktraining.com
eMind - http://www.emind.com
Eno.com - http://www.eno.com/catalog/curriculum.html
Enterprise Training Solutions - http://www.enterprisetraining.com
EuroLearning - http://www.eurolearning.com/UK/main.jsp
Family University - http://www.web-edu.com/fmu/
Fathom - http://www.fathom.com
FindTutorials - http://www.findtutorials.com/
Georgia GLOBE - http://www.georgiaglobe.org
HeadLight.com - http://www.headlight.com
How To Master - http://www.howtomaster.com
Hungry Minds - http://www.hungryminds.com
iclasses.net - http://www.iclasses.net
Ilasallecampus - http://www.ilasallecampus.com/cvf3/Framestruc-
    ture.html
ilearn-nti.com - http://www.ilearn-nti.com/index.html
iLearn.To - http://www.ilearn.to
Inter College - http://intercollege.co.uk
Internet Learning Business School - http://www.ilbsnz.com
Internet U - http://www.internetu.com
Internet University - http://www.internet-university.com
iStudySmart.com - http://www.istudysmart.com/
Jumpstart - http://www.jumpstart.com.sg
Knowledge Anywhere - http://www.knowledgeanywhere.com
KnowledgePlatform.com - http://www.knowledgeplatform.com
KnowledgePool - http://eu.knowledgepool.com/
Learn.com - http://www.learn.com
Learn2.com - http://www.learn2.com/index.asp
Learndirect - http://www.learndirect.co.uk
LearnOnline - http://www.noncredited.net
Limu - http://www.limu.com/

MindEdge – http://www.mindedge.com

Mindleaders – http://www.mindleaders.com

miStupid.com – http://miStupid.com

National College – http://www.nationalcollege.ca

Online College – http://www.theonlinecollege.co.uk

OnlineLearning.net – http://www.onlinelearning.net/

Online University International – http://www.online-university-international.com

OnlineVarsity – http://www.onlinevarsity.com

OurTrainingSite.com – http://www.ourtrainingsite.com

PallasLearning – http://www.pallaslearning.com

PDH Center – http://www.pdhcenter.com

Pentalearn – http://www.pentalearn.com

RedVector.com – http://www.redvector.com

RFP Learning Exchange – http://www.thinq.com/rfpsearch/rfp_us.htm

SmartForce – http://www.smartforce.com

SQLeCenter – http://www.sqlecenter.com

SyberWorks – http://www.syberworks.com/courses.htm

Syntrio – http://www.syntrio.com

TalentEd Virtual Enrichment Program – http://scs.une.edu.au/tedvep/

Thinq.com – http://www.thinq.com

ThirdAge School of Online Learning – http://www.thirdage.com/learning/

Tokono – http://www.groomed.net

Training Department.com – http://www.trainingdepartment.com/

TrainingA – http://www.traininga.com

TrainingNet – http://www.trainingnet.com

Tutor2u – http://www.tutor2u.net

Tutor4Computer.com – http://www.tutor4computer.com

UniversalClass – http://research.universalclass.com

Virtual Training Company (VTC) – http://www.vtc.com/

WebCourse – http://www.webcourse.net

WebCT – http://www.webct.com/wyw/home/

Webotheque – http://www.webotheque.be

World Wide Learn – http://www.worldwidelearn.com/

Youachieve – http://www.youachieve.com

Ten Steps to Making E-Training and Development Work

» Identify the knowledge, skills, and attitudes needed for the organization to achieve its mission and goals.
» Carry out a training and development needs analysis and establish the training and development gap.
» Decide on the means.
» Prepare individual and team training and development plans.
» Make the business case for e-training and development.
» Identify training providers.
» Evaluate success.
» Brief trainees.
» Deliver the training and development.
» Make e-training lifelong training.

1. IDENTIFY THE KNOWLEDGE, SKILLS, AND ATTITUDES NEEDED FOR THE ORGANIZATION TO ACHIEVE ITS MISSION AND GOALS

Training and development are core elements of your business strategy. Successful e-training lines up intellectual capital with business strategy. It combines learning and communication with the Internet to link together diverse processes and knowledge across an extended enterprise – employees, partners, and customers – to achieve organizational dexterity and speed, cost efficiencies, and improvements in quality, performance, and relationships.

The starting point in the process is to meet with managers to discuss their business goals and objectives and how training will support them. Gather sample documents and business examples to use in designing the training so that it relates to the jobs in hand. Ask managers and learners how the training and materials can be designed to best meet their needs.

2. CARRY OUT A TRAINING AND DEVELOPMENT NEEDS ANALYSIS AND ESTABLISH THE TRAINING AND DEVELOPMENT GAP

Once you know the skills, attributes, attitudes, and abilities required to meet the organization's goals, then the next logical step is to find out the current state of human resources. If this has not been done during routine performance appraisals then it will have to be done as a one-off exercise before training and development can commence.

Don't forget that people don't stay put for very long. On average, people stay with one employer for less than 10 years, and in some industries five might be closer to the norm. So you have to allow for that in your thinking and you could consider building into the recruiter's job specification any new skills required.

3. DECIDE ON THE MEANS

The worrying number to remember here is that less than 30% of trainees complete a typical e-training program and achieve the desired output. To overcome the fickleness of e-learners you will have to design content to be as interesting as possible. Based on your budget, media format, and bandwidth, choose among video, audio, digital photos, animations, drawings, and clip art to capture the learner's attention. When it come to clip art, do try not to confine your training program usage to that which can be found on a standard PowerPoint program. Good though these are, they are unlikely to provoke surprise, and surprise is a useful way to maintain interest over the life of a program. Involve the learners by including thought-provoking questions, case studies, surveys, analogies, quizzes, and tests.

Include real-world examples from your business environment – photos, sample documents, charts, interviews, and so forth, will all help to make the content more relevant to the job and hence be more likely to be used and useful.

Build in practice time as each new concept is presented. Include assessment questions after each major concept to test for understanding throughout, not just at the end. Create case studies or scenarios in which learners are asked to apply the knowledge and skills learned rather than just demonstrate recall. Look back and see how IBM got started.

Use a blended approach. Just because you are using e-training doesn't mean you have to throw out tried and proven classroom methods. Put the learning methods to the tasks they are best suited to. Decide which parts of the curriculum need to be offered asynchronously, synchronously, and face-to-face. Consider whether topics need in-person interaction and support (face-to-face), require guided instruction and facilitation (synchronous e-learning), or can be done independently with minimal support (asynchronous e-learning).

Create a curriculum of courses rather than one long master-course designed to teach all people all things. Divide material into modules that can be completed in less than 30 minutes, but include some longer and shorter modules too for those occasions when learners have more or less time to devote to their studies. Be sure to specify how each piece of learning fits in with the others and what essentials are needed before completing each section.

4. PREPARE INDIVIDUAL AND TEAM TRAINING AND DEVELOPMENT PLANS

Break down the curriculum into concise skills based on job needs. Be sure to relate each training skill to a job skill. List objectives in terms of skills, not prior courses taken. For example, rather than stating that an introduction to Microsoft Access course is a prerequisite to the training, list the skills the learners must have mastered, such as creating a database, carrying out a query, preparing a report, and so forth.

Assign students to teams. Linking students to each other helps link them to the course. Some people think e-learning is a solitary endeavor, but it doesn't have to be. It is beneficial for students to give them plenty of group work and encouraging their participation in online discussions.

5. MAKE THE BUSINESS CASE FOR E-TRAINING AND DEVELOPMENT

An e-training and development strategy will require budget allocation. Whilst you will already have a training and development budget, that should not prevent you making the business case for using the "e-route." The following points help to justify such expenditure.

» E-learning is more efficient. It has been shown that learning time can be reduced by as much as 75% when using e-learning, compared to traditional classroom methods. Cutting out "dead time," such as delegate introductions and lunch breaks, reduces learning time. Learners can also skip through or omit material they already know, are not held up when others need more time to grasp the content, and can move at a quicker pace through instructional material, rather than having to follow a trainer's formal scripted presentation.

» E-learning is quicker to deliver. A trainer may typically be able to train only one or two groups per week, and if the group is large it may well take months to complete or hold the organization back if a quicker delivery is required. Also, over long periods of time, the content may change and without a formula for providing quick updates, by the end of the training period out-of-date content could be being delivered. E-learning can be delivered to tens or even hundreds of people at one time. The often higher development costs for e-learning are far outweighed by the delivery cost savings. The savings from delivering e-learning compared to a more traditional approach are so significant that initial outlays are often incidental when the project is viewed as a whole over its entire lifespan.

» Perhaps the greatest cost savings are in the form of opportunity costs, from keeping the employee longer on the job. Taking a salary of $20,000, with the employee working 225 days a year, the average daily cost to the organization (excluding other benefits) is $89. Therefore, a typical five-day course costs the organization $444 in terms of lost productivity at the very least, even before the employees' outputs are taken into account. If this training can be reduced to as little as three days of e-learning, then the immediate productivity gain is at least equivalent to the additional two days the person will be back on the job, i.e. $178. If 2000 people need to receive this training, then the total savings will be $356,000, certainly enough to pay for a reasonably sophisticated program of e-learning solutions. You should also consider that, by training more people more quickly, the implementation of whatever is being taught will be much more rapid, filtering through to increased productivity for the whole initiative. If there were a high turnover of staff, then if the same training could be used year after year, the savings would be even higher.

» If you design the e-learning using easily reusable learning objects, the basic framework could last for many years. Amortising the costs over such a relatively long time period would certainly make an "e-solution" an attractive investment for most training and development activities.

6. IDENTIFY TRAINING PROVIDERS

Many companies outsource portions of their e-learning to one or more suppliers, opting to buy or lease content, infrastructure, or services, rather than create them. The supplier market is consolidating and changing rapidly so it pays to research the market rigorously. As a minimum, compare the cost, effectiveness, scale, and pricing of various e-learning solutions. A comprehensive e-learning system will have one or more of the following components: a learning management system to contain and facilitate e-learning content; tools for creating and managing content and curricula; directive tools for assessment, testing, skill-gap analysis, certification, and tracking; matchmaking tools that can connect learning resources with employees' needs; and tools that can push customized content to people depending on their performance needs, available connectivity, and preferred learning modes.

When you have chosen a supplier, maintain a single point of contact – a project manager. Although each side typically has many team members contributing to the project, miscommunication becomes likely when several individuals are talking within different levels of each organization. Hold frequent progress meetings. Adhering to this simple rule helps improve communication and teamwork on a project. Ideally, once a week at a pre-scheduled time, the vendor and client project managers should discuss the project status, in person or on the phone.

7. EVALUATE SUCCESS

Kirkpatrick's four levels of evaluation (reaction, learning, behavior, results) are ingrained in the training culture and have been covered in this book. But to get the widest acceptance for e-training and development, you will need to go one further and keep in mind Hamblin's fifth level: "ultimate value – has the training helped the organization meet its strategic mission and goals?"

Managers of a business care about results of the business: money, time, and impact. They care less about happy-sheets and course evaluations. They want to do things better, faster, cheaper, easier. Which of e-learning's potential strengths could help achieve this? Is it global consistency of content? Is it learners being able to learn at the most convenient time and place? Is it learners being able to learn just the modules they need? Is it the easier identification of who has what competencies? Is it the opportunity to test and require mastery? Is it the use of simulation? Is it having access to a wide range of outside content? Is it some other capability or feature of e-learning?

This doesn't mean you shouldn't also track trainees and check-in with them regularly. Online trainees can easily lie low, so monitoring their progress is crucial. Check whether trainees return assignments on time and contact them if they haven't, and use a course-management system to track how long trainees stay online.

8. BRIEF TRAINEES

One aspect missing from many training and development programs is the pre-training briefing. Whilst the management team may be fully aware of the organization's future needs in terms of skills, attitudes and abilities, those being trained may be less clear.

So the business case has to be transformed into a personal case. The relationship between the employees' current and future prospects need to be explained in terms of their current skill levels and the levels they will achieve once they have successfully completed the training program.

9. DELIVER THE TRAINING AND DEVELOPMENT

Successful training delivery is an operational matter. You need to make sure the facilities, in terms of access to the Internet or intranet, are made available at appropriate times. People traveling off-site, both locally and internationally, have to be brought into the equation. After all, that is one of the key features of e-learning. It is 24/7, anytime, anywhere, anyhow. But it will only be so if you plan it to be so. In the early days of CBT and CD-ROM training, access to hardware was almost always a bottleneck. Today, with widespread access to computers and the Internet, either using laptops, Internet cafés, or hotel facilities, there is really no reason why someone should miss out on a training assignment. With m-learning there will be even fewer reasons for falling behind with the learning schedule.

10. MAKE E-TRAINING LIFELONG TRAINING

The more varied the ways in which you use e-learning tools and technologies, the more accepted e-learning will become as a standard corporate practice and the more efficient it will be. The goal should be to get e-learning ingrained into the culture so it becomes part of lifelong learning.

Everett Rogers, Regius Professor at the University of New Mexico, spent decades studying the adoption of innovations in organizations around the globe and he identified the following five factors that pull adopters toward innovations.

1 **Advantage** – the new thing has to be better than other alternatives.
2 **Compatibility** – the new thing has to feel familiar and fit my beliefs.
3 **Simplicity** – the new thing has to be simple to use.
4 **Trialability** – the new thing has to be easy to try.
5 **Observability** – I have to be able to see other people's positive results from it.

IBM has applied Rogers' concepts to its management development e-learning effort as follows.

1 **Advantage** – IBM management development offers "quick-views," instant online briefings on 40-plus leadership and people-management topics. They are easy to access, available as and when needed, and allow classroom sessions to focus on discussion rather than presenting information.

2 **Compatibility** – IBM management development Websites replicate the look and feel of Lotus Notes, the standard IBM interface.

3 **Simplicity** – IBM management development Websites require no plug-ins. Ease of use is the top priority in design.

4 **Trialability** – IBM management development allows free access to all Websites without passwords or personal tracking so that learners feel safe and comfortable.

5 **Observability** – IBM management development implemented quick-views first so that learners would experience immediate solutions to practical problems. If you can set out to follow Rogers' rules by making e-learning easy to adopt, then you too could make e-training a lifelong experience.

KEY LEARNING POINTS

» Identify the knowledge, skills, and attitudes needed for the organization to achieve its mission and goals.
» Carry out a training and development needs analysis and establish the training and development gap.
» Decide on the means.
» Prepare individual and team training and development plans.
» Make the business case for e-training and development.
» Identify training providers.
» Evaluate success.
» Brief trainees.
» Deliver the training and development.
» Make e-training lifelong training.

Frequently Asked Questions (FAQ)s

Q1: What is e-training and development?
A: See Chapter 1 for an introduction and Chapter 2 for some definitions.

Q2: Why should I bother with e-training and development?
A: See Chapter 7 for some real-life success stories and Chapter 4 for a look at how e-training and development is viewed.

Q3: Is e-training and development really any different from training and development?
A: See Chapter 2 for a comparison with conventional training and development.

Q4: How long has e-training and development been around and where did it come from?
A: See Chapter 3 for a look at how e-training and development has evolved.

Q5: I would like to introduce e-training and development. How should I go about it?

A: See Chapter 10 for 10 practical steps to making it work and the case studies in Chapter 7 on how it's actually been done by various organizations.

Q6: Is there a body of theory to support the arguments for e-training and development?

A: See Chapter 8 for a look at some key thinkers and related concepts, and Chapter 5, which deals with the global dimension.

Q7: How can I find out more about the subject and get some help?

A: See Chapter 9 for a comprehensive list of resources.

Q8: Anything to do with the Internet is always full of jargon. How can I find out what terms such as "asynchronous" and "learning management system" mean?

A: See Chapter 8 for a glossary of terms.

Q9: I would like to test out some ready-made e-training and development packages, preferably at little or no cost. How would I go about that?

A: See the e-learning portals listed in Chapter 9 for a good starting point.

Q10: How can I make sure any investment I make in this area will be effective?

A: See Chapter 4 on making e-training and development successful, tracking (training's missing link), and a best practice case study (US West).

Index

EXPRESSEXEC –
BUSINESS THINKING AT YOUR FINGERTIPS

ExpressExec is a 12-module resource with 10 titles in each module. Combined they form a complete resource of current business practice. Each title enables the reader to quickly understand the key concepts and models driving management thinking today.

Innovation

01.01 *Innovation Express*
01.02 *Global Innovation*
01.03 *E-Innovation*
01.04 *Creativity*
01.05 *Technology Leaders*
01.06 *Intellectual Capital*
01.07 *The Innovative Individual*
01.08 *Taking Ideas to Market*
01.09 *Creating an Innovative Culture*
01.10 *Managing Intellectual Property*

Enterprise

02.01 *Enterprise Express*
02.02 *Going Global*
02.03 *E-Business*
02.04 *Corporate Venturing*
02.05 *Angel Capital*
02.06 *Managing Growth*
02.07 *Exit Strategies*
02.08 *The Entrepreneurial Individual*
02.09 *Business Planning*
02.10 *Creating the Entrepreneurial Organization*

Strategy

03.01 *Strategy Express*
03.02 *Global Strategy*
03.03 *E-Strategy*
03.04 *The Vision Thing*
03.05 *Strategies for Hypergrowth*
03.06 *Complexity and Paradox*
03.07 *The New Corporate Strategy*
03.08 *Balanced Scorecard*
03.09 *Competitive Intelligence*
03.10 *Future Proofing*

Marketing

04.01 *Marketing Express*
04.02 *Global Marketing*
04.03 *E-Marketing*
04.04 *Customer Relationship Management*
04.05 *Reputation Management*
04.06 *Sales Promotion*
04.07 *Channel Management*
04.08 *Branding*
04.09 *Market Research*
04.10 *Sales Management*

Finance

05.01 *Finance Express*
05.02 *Global Finance*
05.03 *E-Finance*
05.04 *Investment Appraisal*
05.05 *Understanding Accounts*
05.06 *Shareholder Value*
05.07 *Valuation*
05.08 *Strategic Cash Flow Management*
05.09 *Mergers and Acquisitions*
05.10 *Risk Management*

Operations and Technology

06.01 *Operations and Technology Express*
06.02 *Operating Globally*
06.03 *E-Processes*
06.04 *Supply Chain Management*
06.05 *Crisis Management*
06.06 *Project Management*
06.07 *Managing Quality*
06.08 *Managing Technology*
06.09 *Measurement and Internal Audit*
06.10 *Making Partnerships Work*

Available from:
www.expressexec.com

Customer Service Department
John Wiley & Sons Ltd
Southern Cross Trading Estate
1 Oldlands Way, Bognor Regis
West Sussex, PO22 9SA
Tel: +44(0)1243 843 294
Fax: +44(0)1243 843 303
Email: cs-books@wiley.co.uk

Printed and bound by CPI Group (UK) Ltd, Croydon, CR0 4YY

14/04/2025

14656896-0001